THE BAFFLER

WINTER 1999   NUMBER

TABLE OF CONTENTS

The

BAFFLER

Editor
Thomas Frank

Managing Editor
"Diamonds" Dave Mulcahey

Associate Editors
Michael Szalay, Matt Weiland

Fiction Editor
Gwenan Wilbur

Poetry Editors
Damon Krukowski, Jennifer Moxley

Publisher
Greg Lane

Contributing Editors
**Chris Lehmann, Kim Phillips-Fein,
Tom Vanderbilt**

Associate Publisher
Emily Vogt

Publishing Assistants
Amanda Klonsky, Kristie Lynne Reilly

Hodakting Editors
George Hodak, Jim McNeill

Founders
Thomas Frank, Keith White

THE BAFFLER wishes to thank Mike O'Flaherty, Kristen Lehner, Bill Ayers, Judith Kirshner, Ryan P. Jackson, and Dan Raeburn.

The complete texts of Noah Warren-Mann's articles and sundry other documents appear on THE BAFFLER's Web site. TRI's Web site is http://members.tripod.com/~teloprex.

We completed this BAFFLER in October 1999. Subscriptions to THE BAFFLER cost $24 for four issues and can be purchased by check at the address below, or by credit card at thebaffler.com and 1-888-387-8947. The editors invite submissions of art, fiction, and essays. All submissions must be accompanied by a stamped, addressed envelope. Submissions should be addressed to the Editor and not to individuals. Unsolicited poetry submissions will not be considered or returned. All requests for permissions and reprints must be made in writing to the Publisher. Six weeks advance notice is required for changes of address.

All correspondence should be sent to the address below.

This issue: The conservative "years in the wilderness." You've heard about them, right? Back when tory's only comfort was the Hearst Newspapers, the Gannett Newspapers, the *Chicago Tribune*, the National Association of Manufacturers, the American Legion, the Liberty League, America First, every advertising agency and country club and investment bank in the land. Back when people—so unfairly!—associated pro-business politics with the interests of the well-to-do. Sad, tough times indeed. Everybody had to wear dark, scratchy suits. There were no happy brands. Weep with us. Next issue: Watch the blueboys at the top of their form! See them conquer the citadels of state on behalf of an aggrieved public, a public that demands: Bring back our corporations! Marvel as a "New Paradigm" makes all previous history meaningless—as the leftist media conspiracy is exposed—as the "limousine liberals" are finally put in their place and all things are made good and right and fine and the people clenches its jaw and is bathed in fine golden forgetfulness!

Just don't let that stock market do anything bad until we're done.

P.O. Box 378293, Chicago, Ills. 60637 · thebaffler.com

LEGIONNAIRE'S DISEASE

THOMAS FRANK

IT'S NOT difficult to understand the sense of historical frustration that informs so much of the bitter populism of recent decades. We, too, regret many of the ways the world has changed over the last thirty years; we, too, believe that the vast majority of Americans have good reason to be angry over the way they have been done over; and we, too, have little patience for ten-minute drum solos.

But what makes us stand back and gape in awe at the thirty-year ascendancy of backlash politics—stretching as they have from the day Chicago nightstick struck hippie skull to the recent impeachment fiasco—is the cultural accomplishment of the thing. How did the bunch of privileged former frat boys, lawyers, and corporate officers who staffed the Nixon, Reagan, and Gingrich revolutions ever come to convince themselves, let alone an entire nation, that they spoke on behalf of the People and that they were the victims of some kind of elitist conspiracy? How did they continue to impress voters with the threat posed by the liberal state long after liberals had disappeared from the national stage? And how were they able to persuade Americans that those few summers of boomer joy back in the Sixties required thirty years of payback?

These are the questions that this issue of THE BAFFLER proposes to investigate, largely by turning to the prehistory of the backlash ascendancy, by examining the personalities and movements and ideas that made right-wing populism possible.

For the kind of "middle American" figures who populated the Midwestern suburbia of my youth, the answers were self-evident. Something had gone so wildly wrong for them in the Sixties—and had stayed so steadfastly wrong ever since—that nothing could ever make them whole again. Their favorite magazines, radio hosts, and politicians would never let them forget it, either, dangling before them an ever-growing list of impossible grievances against the world: tales of welfare degeneracy, crime in the streets, crazy civil rights leaders, obscene art, foolish professors, or sitcom provocations, each one, without fail, producing the desired result. Which is not to say that the professors resigned, or that the sitcoms failed, but that the "middle Americans" grew ever more bitter, ever more certain that the entire world of expertise—the media, the judges, the psychologists, the academics, the politicians—had entered into a conspiracy against their way of life.

On the other hand, many of these backlash subjects were successful people, self-made men who had done well in their fields of banking and clerking and sales—the sort of folks who are supposed to regard American life with optimism and satisfaction, not infinite bitterness. What's more, the politicians that so wound them up won virtually every election, fashioning the never-ebbing mad-as-hellness of millions of bitter self-made men into an unstoppable electoral coalition. And yet nothing could assuage their fury. However righteously Reagan might drone, however boldly Bush might pose with the flag or Gingrich snarl at those elitist "McGoverniks," the culture wars they declared were always lost, and the age of polite consensus and public decency grew ever further out of reach. "America is Back!" they crowed proudly after electing some reactionary or another, only to sink back into bitterness the next day: America is *never* back, it is *always* betrayed, *every time* those Sixties people sneak in the back door and ruin everything.

But the strangest fantasy of all behind the thirty-year backlash had to do with social class. As Barbara Ehrenreich demonstrated in *Fear of Falling*, still the definitive treatment of the subject, conservatives solved the problems of the Sixties by "rediscovering" the working class and attributing to it all manner of "family values" sentiments. Between the 1969 flurry over reactionary "hardhats," Nixon's salutes to the hardworking Silent Majority, and the liberals' shameful acceptance of the new stereotype (cf., Archie Bunker), they were able to balance out the authenticity of the civil rights and antiwar movements with the authenticity of the working class. While those crazy kids ran wild in the streets, real Americans went to church and defended their flag.

Never mind for now that the story wasn't true (as Ehrenreich points out, working Americans actually remained consistently liberal throughout the period in question): For the bitter self-made men of my acquaintance it fit the picture perfectly. They themselves were members of the universal and hard-bitten proletariat of taxpayers, they imagined, and they understood their fight with the world as an oddly jiggered sort of class war, a battle in which class was a cultural issue rather than a material one, a question of right thinking rather than of ownership, a confrontation with pretentiousness and permissiveness rather than poverty. What's more, there were always enough hardhat types around to make the fantasy plausible, enough unions that valued culture war sufficiently to endorse Ronald Reagan for president.

In the end the series of culture warriors they helped elect turned out to care far more about freeing the corporations than bringing back the Fifties or abolishing art. As it turned out, culture war was always more about *managing* the beloved blue-collar class than *appealing* to it. The further back one looks in the history of right-wing populism, the more layers of varnish that are stripped away, the clearer this becomes.

Came for the Americanism, Stayed for the Strikebreaking

SOME who lived through it understood the First World War as a colossal exercise in futility, the dead end where the

reer as America's most prominent red-hunter), the Legionnaires fought for a world that worked the way normal people wanted it to. They warred on immigrants, on insufficiently American schoolteachers, on "alien slackers," on the ACLU, on "cosmopolitans," on the red universities, on public speakers with whom they disagreed, on virtually every aspect of the cultural and political ferment of the preceding thirty years. Whether running radicals out of town or urging the establishment of red-hunting committees in Congress, the Legion claimed to speak for an average America beyond both the "classes and the masses," daring to pronounce the truths that legal procedure and democratic niceties ordinarily forbade.

Western world's hollow verities seemed to collapse once and for all. The former soldiers who formed the American Legion in 1919, however, sincerely believed that the Great War was all it had been advertised to be. For them a few years of trench warfare affirmed the truth of the old slogans and patriotic phrases so persuasively and so conclusively that within months after coming back from France they met in convention and declared a culture war for the very soul of their nation. It was a Pentecost of ordinariness: The boys were back to purify their own land, to elevate the flag to a higher plane of symbolism, to speak every one of them in the highfalutin tongues of red-hot patriotism. Led by the sons of prominent politicians both Republican and Democratic, backed enthusiastically by captains of industry and the governors of many states, and marching under the banner of "100 percent Americanism," a phrase conjured up for them by Hamilton Fish (soon to begin his ca-

Intellectuals of the era laughed the Legion off. In the novels of the Jazz Age they were depicted as comic reactionaries, bellowing boobs in Sam Browne belts whose disapproval was a coveted prize—much in the way contemporary artists vie to win the antagonism of Jesse Helms or contemporary advertising establishes a product's quality by showing how it pisses off the suits. In the industrial wars of that period, though, the Legion's contributions were less comical. They contributed mightily to the great red roundup of 1919 and even shot it out in places with their archenemy, the IWW. They furnished strikebreakers at many of the confrontations of the Twenties and Thirties and developed an obsessive anticommunism that would, some thirty years later, metastasize into a full-blown society-wide paranoia.

In its early days the Legion embodied many of the characteristics that historian Michael Kazin associates with American populism: the concern with "Americanism" and, more crucially, with identifying and fighting "un-American" ideas and organizations; a notion of "the people" in all their glorious averageness; and above all a sense of crisis, of the Republic imperiled by some implacable elitist foe, in this case the partisans of the treasonous "isms" that the Legion seemed to find lurking everywhere.

By today's standards, though, a better term than "populism" would be "whip hand of capital." While Legion doctrine depicted the organization as a bridge between the classes, it was also the brainchild of a handful of high-ranking officers and businessmen (including "Wild Bill" Donovan, future head of the OSS) who spoke of their creation as a weapon in the class war they believed was impending. Some Legion leaders openly equated their group with the Italian Fascists; anticommunist historian Richard Gid Powers goes as far as to assert that the Legion was modeled on the proto-Nazi Freikorps, then running rampant throughout Germany.

Either way, the owner community liked what it saw. The young organization was bankrolled by prominent corporations just as interested in combating rampant radicalism as were the millionaire colonels who established the group in the first place. Legion leaders returned the favor in the Thirties, stoutly backing the National Association of Manufacturers (NAM) as it cranked up its own culture war on the New Deal and sought to tag

economic regulation as the first step down the road to tyranny.

That particular offensive never got very far, of course. Despite the NAM's and the Legion's fantasies of a common people outraged at a grasping octopus state, few in the Thirties were actually persuaded to view the corporations as trustees of the general will. That delusion would have to wait many years before it found a receptive audience, years after the Legion had made its peace with the welfare state (it lobbied heavily for the GI Bill of Rights), dropped the paramilitary act, and become centrist and inoffensive. For the last thirty years, though, we have all of us been living in the Legion's world, a place where epidemic violations of the principles of "Americanism" bring on wave after wave of popular indignation— and in which the nation's owners are showered by grateful legislators with gift after gift.

Taps

BUT that, thankfully, is beginning to change at last. A recent replaying of TV news coverage from 1980 reminds us how far we have come: To cover the interminable hostage crisis of that year the reporters went through all of the standard populist motions of the day, including conducting interviews with angry blue-collar men in a barber shop somewhere in deepest America. (Naturally, the men whose testimony was aired were inconsolably bitter about national decline, believing the absolute worst about everyone concerned.) In 1980 such footage was a standard element of any national TV news program. It's inconceivable today. Not only have blue-collar organizations dropped off the face of the media earth, but the salty affirmations of their members are no longer required. They count for nothing either as an economic force or as a repository of authenticity.

Ironically, such figures essentially negated themselves. The backlash they symbolized made the Reagan revolution possible; as it in turn gave rise to the New Economy, it has brought with it a new species of self-justification, one with little need for the sanction of "middle Americans" or anybody else. The great thinkers of the right have looked around them and decided that the way of the free market is not just profitable, it's the very crown of creation, the inevitable result of centuries of global progress. The corporations aren't ruling on behalf of some "silent majority" or even Newt Gingrich's "normal Americans"; these days it's the future, it's the entire planet that is said to have endorsed the Wall Street way.

Not only is global inevitability a more flattering idea for columnists and think-tankers than reaction ever was, but it also promises to tame the hardhatted beast far more effectively than thirty years of AM radio and wedge-issue divisiveness. Last Labor Day, just about the only time when union spokesmen are permitted to violate the free-market consensus that reigns across the channels of responsible

commentary, AFL-CIO Secretary-Treasurer Richard Trumka appeared on *Crossfire* to take on a Republican congressional firebrand. The program's right-wing host, Mary Matalin, guided the conversation unfailingly down the familiar pathways of backlash sentiment, announcing first that she was one with the "working stiff"—a member, in fact, of no fewer than three unions!—and then joining forces with the congressman to berate Trumka for the usual bill of grievances. How could the AFL-CIO support so many Democrats and such a liberal agenda, they demanded, when polls revealed that many union members were in

RADIO TO SPIKE RUSSIAN SLURS ON U.S. WOMEN

CARTOONIST, STUDENT RESCUED AFTER CANOE CAPSIZES IN LAKE

ANIMAL PETS GO TO CHURCH; HEAR ABOUT HEAVEN

——— WE THINK YOU'LL LIKE ———

fact family-values mini-Reagans? Trumka, though, refused to budge, pointing out simply that some legislation was better for the rich than for workers, that Republican leaders had repeatedly called for a national right-to-work law and had even spoken enthusiastically of union-busting. When taunted with the routine charge that union wages are disproportionately high, this back-talking ingrate even dared to point out the vast differential between CEO salaries and those of their workers. As soon as he had left the set, though, Matalin had her revenge. If workers were no longer going to play their appointed part in the backlash, then who needed them? The New Economy had no place for such as Trumka: "You can't stop globalization any more than you can stop computers," she smugged.

Nor does the New Economy have much use for that other backlash subject, the bitter self-made men. Once they were the toast of Limbaugh and *Reader's Digest*, the sort of realistic, down-to-earth guys who knew that you had to fight for every dollar and who took no nonsense, either from employees or government. But who gives a damn about them now? While they were getting worked up at the do-goodery of the milquetoast liberals, their pals in the Fortune 500 were deciding that they, too, had had enough of the "angry white male." Today the corporate imagination is fired by crazy makers of wow and zany change agents. The fantasy subject of the New Economy is not some hardened doubter; it's a kid with a goatee who's just IPO'd and who's now being celebrated in Dodge commercials, Arthur Andersen ads, and *Fortune* magazine cover stories. As the secretary of the treasury dotingly describes him, he's "made his first hundred million before he's bought his first suit," he's a "visionary entrepreneur" just out of college, he plays hackysack in the aisle of his Lear jet. If "100 percent Americanism" means anything to him, it's the new corporate fantasy of "Free Agent Nation," a place where bosses have finally been freed from the bonds of loyalty to anyone and the funky tastes of the counterculture are recognized as markers of entrepreneurial prowess.

So hail and farewell, Legionnaires and bitter self-made men. You have done your historical duty ably, rescued your employers from the dark decades of regulation and taxation, and delivered your nation into the hands of a higher order of men, a race of seers mystically attuned to the divine rhythms of the market. They owe you a debt of thanks, all you hardhats, you believers, you Reagan Democrats, you Middle Americans. For the rich you have truly made it "Morning in America." It was your rage against authority that gave us the Cato Institute, your refusal to be ruled that built us a Bill Gates, your fury against those smelly hippies that has sent all those IPO kids on their snowboarding vacations to Gstaad. But as your beloved hometowns sink silently into the special oblivion the global marketplace has reserved for them, as you flip the pages of *Modern Maturity* and wonder why your health care sucks so, as your way of life comes to an unsung end and your kids get turned down by the private schools you no longer have any hope of affording, somehow we doubt that there will be too many monuments to honor your achievement. Let this BAFFLER be your marker, your cenotaph.

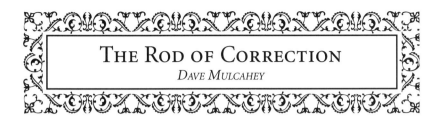

THE ROD OF CORRECTION
DAVE MULCAHEY

IN JUNE 1968 the world was in flames. The Vietcong had recently overrun Saigon, American cities smoldered in the aftermath of the King riots, and the Yippies were threatening to drop acid in Chicago's water supply. Readers of that month's *Reader's Digest* learned how to cope with this bummer from a curious yarn titled "I Will Not Let You Steal My Shoes." It recounted the fateful tryst of one W. N. Templeton and a slender girl called Gazelle. As Templeton strolled at twilight on a Moroccan beach with this oddly named mignonne (a Basque colonist with "a gypsy beauty about her"), the couple was set upon by three knife-wielding Arabs. This was 1955, short on the heels of a nasty anticolonial revolt, and Templeton knew well that "the instigators of terrorist activities against France" had inflamed Moroccan peasants with "talk of Holy War." Premonitions of rape and grisly knifeplay danced in Templeton's head. He regretted that he hadn't packed his revolver. Presently, the leader of the gang grabbed at Gazelle's sandals, which she held in her hand. But Gazelle, it turned out, knew a thing or two about how to deal with terrorists: She did not let go but fixed the brute with a gaze of self-possessed determination. No dice on the shoes, she informed him, because "if I allow you to rob me, I help you to become a thief." And Gazelle wasn't the kind of soon-to-be-dispossessed *colon* who turns the subjected Other into a thief. "Torture us, kill us, if you want," Gazelle continued in Franco-Arabic patois, but understand that to do so would be cowardly, since we're unarmed and this man is a visitor from across the seas. Remember, Allah sees everything, and He never forgives cowards. Here, I *give* you my sandals!

That clinched it. As Templeton looked on with wonder, Gazelle's plucky little sermon reduced the ruffians to tears. They dropped their knives (which "met the sand with a zinging sound"). Thug No. 1 looked up at Gazelle. "There was no longer defiance in [his eyes]," Templeton noticed. "[R]ather, I saw a glimmer of the kindly dignity which is the mark of the Moroccan peasant." Before disappearing with his confederates over a dune, the repentant thief gave this benediction: "Go in peace. Allah guards you." We learn in the last line of the story that Templeton made Gazelle his wife. As for the would-be robbers, lives of kindly dignity no doubt awaited them.

For all we know, a sylph named Gazelle may have lived in Casablanca in the Fifties, and she may have faced down a band of menacing Maghrebis. My money, however, says that "W. N. Templeton" was no South African automobile importer, as his biographical squib purported, but a *Digest* staffer, or maybe a CIA functionary exploring his literary side. The possibility can't be ruled out that he was all three, but in the end questions of authorship, or of veracity, are irrelevant. Published just five months after the Tet Offensive, which dramatically shattered the illusion that American forces had the Vietnam War well in hand, the point of Templeton's parable could not have been lost on many of the magazine's tens of millions of readers: In the thankless business of administering civilization to nonwestern peoples, you win some and you lose some. You may even have to return countries to their rightful owners, but you should never, ever let them forget who's boss.

The story fit nicely alongside the *Digest*'s other coverage of the war: implausibly upbeat stories ("What Does Combat Do to Our Men?"—it teaches them valuable leadership skills and makes them fine citizens), sensational accounts of enemy cruelty ("The Blood-Red Hands of Ho Chi Minh"), and exhortations to give Charlie a taste of our *really* big guns. In its own hamfisted way, the *Digest* strived to live up to the legacy of Lord Northcliffe, founder of the *Daily Mail* and British director of propaganda during the First World War, who boasted, "Journalists are more important to the winning of the war than the generals." It has been well documented that the *Digest*, like certain other large-circulation American periodicals, took CIA, FBI, and State Department

feed for decades—though the ties were usually informal enough to safeguard editorial pretensions of objectivity. During the Second World War, the U.S. government pitched a scheme to sponsor *Digest* editions in Sweden and Latin America as a means to counterbalance Nazi propaganda in those countries. As Peter Canning recounts in *American Dreamers*, his 1996 history of the *Digest*, publisher DeWitt Wallace blanched at the idea of turning his magazine into a propaganda vehicle but went ahead with the editions anyway. It got much worse in the coming decades as the United States embarked on "containment" adventures around the globe. By 1968, Canning wrote, *Digest* honchos were not only working directly with State Department staff on certain war-related stories, but in the case of at least one story—which used a potpourri of reports and speeches from North Vietnam to suggest that antiwar protesters were "giving aid and comfort to the enemy"—galleys were shown only to subeditors considered "politically reliable." In 1977 the *Digest* managed to run the first report in the U.S. press on Pol Pot's murderous campaign in Cambodia. How the *Digest* pulled off this coup when all foreign reporters had been kicked out of the country may be surmised from the bits of CIA disinformation that larded the piece.

But to focus on the *Digest*'s CIA connections is to miss the larger point about its journalistic mission. The secret of the magazine's success was its unshakable faith in uplift and the "home truths" of Wallace's Midwestern Calvinism—admixed, of course, with the sort of hardright politics that made it a favorite among the country's top businessmen,

The Baffler Magazine introduced and urged the observance of "I AM AN AMERICAN" DAY

clergymen, and spooks. It could be counted on to dress up the ruthless reasons of state with sanctimony, sentimentality, and cuteness. Even as it beat the drum for the Taft-Hartley Act and carpet-bombing, the *Digest* never neglected to pass along the

lessons we can learn from our pets, self-abnegating peons, or the terminally ill man who finally caught that big fish. In its seemingly earnest attempts to grapple with the crises of the times, the *Digest* always arrived at a defense of power. In early 1968 it denounced Martin Luther King's program of civil disobedience as a threat to the "basic freedoms" of the land and grist for "Communism's worldwide propaganda apparatus." A few months later, amid the riots following King's assassination, the *Digest* reported that business leaders were healing the nation: "In contrast to the American trade-union movement, which is one of the greatest bastions of racial discrimination in this country, business understands that there are many Negroes, who, with job training, would be good workers—and business needs workers.")

TONIGHT:

Bishop Sheen

Melts Away Mucus and Coughing of

SUPER ANAHIST
NASAL SPRAY

8:30 CHANNEL 7

He looks like the kind of Frenchman I was warned about . . . He's perfect!

LIVE FROM NEW YORK

Like Ronald Reagan, whose unmistakably *Digest*-inspired imbecilities blew one last gust of balmy majoritarianism up the backside of the American body politic, the magazine is a fading relic of a time that now seems quaint and improbable. It stood in the breach to defend a faith now considered absurd even by the sons and daughters of the faithful. As Reagan and the *Digest* fumble toward the grave, we should not underestimate their role in destroying the innocent America they championed. In its zeal to twist any truth to serve the needs of state, the *Digest* did more to foster the cynicism and disbelief it railed against than all the combined scoffing of the Communists, hippies, union chiselers, and Weathermen it so fervidly denounced back in the day.

THE BRAND CALLED SHMOO

LI'L ABNER FROM LEFT TO RIGHT

DAN RAEBURN

ALFRED Caplin emerged from the dim, gray depths of the Great Depression as Al Capp, creator of the beloved hillbilly comic strip *Li'l Abner* and the most celebrated cartoonist of the American century. In the strip's early years, *Li'l Abner* was praised by liberal intellectuals, who saw Capp as a sort of populist knight-errant, the people's own satirist, a witty warrior whose pen punctured the bloated plutocrats lording it over the downtrodden everyman. Years of left populism made Capp a rich, rich man. But by the time his career ended in the early Seventies, Capp had switched sides, becoming the comic Lancelot of the right. He was still praised as a defender of the average man, but now it was the loony, high-horse student left who served as Capp's target, those comfy Ivy Leaguers who rode roughshod (and bareback, naturally) over us humble commoners of the "Silent Majority." Al Capp began his career as the FDR of the funny pages and ended it as their George Wallace.

Or so the story goes. Capp's left-to-right, head-to-tail flip is the standard narrative one encounters in the various biographies of the cartoonist, and the big question raised by Capp's conversion to the right in the Sixties—namely, why did it happen?—is the toss-up put to the reader by Alexander Theroux in his recently published booklet, *The Enigma of Al Capp* (Fantagraphics, 1999). Unfortunately, Theroux never decides exactly why Capp changed sides. He comes closest to a convincing explanation when he focuses, as do all Capp's biographers, on Capp's wooden leg as the man's lifelong curse and a symbol for all the insecurity and resentment his impoverished youth bred in him. Using what we might call the wooden-leg-as-Rosebud theory and running through a list of Capp's other personal disappointments, Theroux essentially retells the usual Capp narrative, that of the eventually curdled sourpuss whose acidic comics were once upon a time sweetened with a little more of the milk of human kindness. According to Theroux, the left lost something great, something almost revolutionary, when it lost Al Capp. "Underneath [*Li'l Abner*'s satire] is social seriousness if not solemnity, and, if it's not an oxymoron, almost Marxist humor," Theroux notes. "It's my belief that the comic strip *Li'l Abner* is one long fable about greed."

To use a word of Capp's own inven-

Dan Raeburn publishes *The Imp*, an annual booklet of comics criticism. He lives in Chicago.

tion, this is hogwash. While it's true that *Li'l Abner* can be read as one long fable about greed, the greed in question was clearly Al Capp's own. As is so often the case, the seemingly irreconcilable left and right sides of Al Capp's politics were really flip sides of our only coin: money.

Like almost everyone else who has written about Capp, Theroux assumes that his subject changed in some fundamental way, and that this is what explains his political shift. But Theroux would have done well to listen more closely to the words of his own subject. Capp himself maintained until the end that he had always been the same man; that society, not him, had changed. Al Capp did not turn into a bitter, greedy asshole in the Sixties—he was *always* a bitter, greedy asshole. Oddly, Theroux presents all the evidence necessary to prove this, but shrinks from drawing the obvious conclusions. In fact, any fairly critical look at Capp's life and a trudge through Capp's alleged "funnies" forces upon one the obvious truth that Capp was not so much a knight but a mercenary in the earliest of the culture wars. Capp himself put it best when asked by a student what exactly had inspired him to begin drawing a comic strip about hillbillies: "Money," he barked.

Despite the intellectual significance once attributed to Capp's awful comic strips, Capp was always a pawn in a larger game. To be sure, he was one of the culture war's first heroes and perhaps its first casualty, but in a larger sense his story is that of the middle class's endless fascination with the authentic, unwashed culture of the common man, of the inflated prices intellectuals will pay for cultural populism of almost any kind. Capp's biogra-

phers tell the story of Al Capp's victory over poverty; they ignore the less obvious story of poverty's victory over Al Capp.

Alfred Gerald Caplin was born in the first years of this century, a poor Jewish boy on the ghetto side of New Haven. Class resentment seems to have dogged him from the beginning. Although his family moved constantly, Alfred grew up always in the metaphorical shadow of Yale, an upper-class fortress that haunted his entire life. When Alfred was nine years old a streetcar ran over him and severed one of his legs. Because Alfred loathed his wooden leg, his friends and brother tugged him in a wagon when they made their self-described "Robin Hood raids" on the local Woolworth's, stealing pocket knives, cheap jewelry, and kewpie dolls. In adolescence Alfred would play the part of a Yalie alter ego he invented, the scruffy-genteel Alfred Von Schuyler, in various ill-fated attempts to seduce powdered and pampered girls from the upper crust. After dropping out of several art schools Alfred began a career as a cartoonist assisting Ham Fisher, creator of *Joe Palooka*. It was during this period of plodding poverty, at the very pit of the Great Depression, that Caplin hit on the idea of making fun of poor people. After he saw a hillbilly revue in a New York vaudeville house, Caplin changed his name to Al Capp and began drawing hillbillies—lazy white people who were poor as dirt, dumb as dirt, and who, like their equally imaginary black counterparts, said "Shonuff." Sure enough, the idea caught on. Al Capp struck gold in them thar hills.

The popularity not just of *Li'l Abner* but of all cartoons in those years is almost inconceivable today. The comics were postwar America's most popular art—as Capp himself noted in an essay he wrote for a supplement to the 1946 *Encyclopædia Britannica*—and by Capp's peak in the early Fifties *Li'l Abner* was the most popular strip of them all. More than ninety million Americans read *Li'l Abner* every single day of their lives; in quantitative terms this made Al Capp the most important artist in America. Only the Beatles' arrival a decade later can compare to the chorus of oohs and aahs that rose and fell with the vacillating fortunes of Capp's cornpone heroes, the Yokum family.

Today, only twenty-five years after his retirement, Capp is largely forgotten and for good reason. The only thing about *Li'l Abner* that is funny now is the fact that so many people once gave a hoot about it. After plowing through all forty-three years of Capp's daily comics—comics consisting almost entirely of vicious burlesques, boilerplate dialogue, and ridiculously

contrived "situation comedy"—one is bored beyond all emotions save irritation. Most irritating of all is Capp's hamhanded use of ethnic stereotypes. Whether it was the Polecat tribe, injuns drunk on Kickapoo Joy Juice (a nonalcoholic version of which Capp marketed, and which is still sold today in parts of the Third World); the "Unteachables" (a mob of greaseball, pinstripe Sicilians); or the snoring meggsican hombres and impossibly oversexed, red hot gorls of El Apassionato, racial caricatures were Capp's forte. In a perhaps intentional show of bogus "integrity," Capp even drew his own people as a tribe of hooknosed shysters.

Capp's main character was Li'l Abner hisself, the proto-Gump and first massmedia imbecile to serve as an emblem of all the lunkheads that the two coasts

imagine to inhabit America's great middle. This Brobdingnagian lummox was "the man with the lowest I.Q. in America." As Capp once crowed, "When Li'l Abner speaks, he speaks for millions of morons." The mate Capp fashioned for Abner was the buxom, brainless Daisy Mae, a naive, chaste, barely clothed shotgun-shack tart who fully, and I do mean fully, embodied the Madonna/whore complex. When not chasing Abner on her fleet bare feet every Sadie Hawkins Day, Daisy Mae was heaven-bent on capturing him for marriage. Capp's idjit Adam and Eve hailed from the mountain hamlet of Dogpatch, U.S.A., a yokel's Yoknapatawpha, a hillbilly Eden where all stayed poor by virtue of their inanity. As the strip's plot unfolded, Abner clodhopped his way across the landscape of American life, exposing folly and avarice wherever he loped—admirers of Capp from Theroux to John Updike refer to Abner as a sort of aw-shucks Candide—and won out in the end by virtue of his stupidity, naiveté, and deep faith in the red, white, and blue. Virtually all of Capp's central cast of characters fit the same profile: lazy, illiterate, barefoot sharecroppers in tattered clothes—charming innocents untouched by sivvylyzashun, mouthing in their every encounter with city folk and all forms of authority a dumb profundity, one all the more compelling for its being untouched by subject-verb agreement. There's something about this formula of average-dope-confronts-power that has always appealed to middle-class Americans, perhaps because, as with the denizens of Dogpatch, these simpleton protagonists are always portrayed as children. No matter what their age, they and their grotesque lumpen brothers in poverty were constantly sleeping, drinking, hoodwinking, and screwing—that last act being of course only suggested, especially on Sadie Hawkins Day. After Li'l Abner finally married Daisy Mae, he got the only job he ever held—a mattress tester. Zzzzz. Natcherly, the Dogpatch crowd were good chilluns, prefacing their address of rich folk with "yassuh," "nossuh," and other markers of old-fashioned deference. What Capp invented was a new kind of minstrelsy, one that did without the basic element previously thought necessary for a minstrel show—namely, black people. For all his nasty stereotyping, Capp's great accomplishment was his bleaching of this all-American form of mockery.

The only experience that approaches the agony of following years of Li'l Abner's picaresque adventures is reading what overeager intellectuals of his time made of these insufferably dumb comics. Believe it or not, they were convinced that Capp was the mythical common man in the flesh, a veritable fount of the vox populi. The dialect of Dogpatch was a particular favorite of these thinkers, the ancestors of today's cult-studs. For Capp's 1953 book, The World of Li'l Abner, John Steinbeck—of all people!—contributed an introduction in which he proclaimed, "I think Capp may very possibly be the best writer in the world today." Steinbeck then recommended that Capp be given the Nobel Prize for literature because, he reasoned, literature is what the people actually read—and everybody read Al Capp. "He has not only invented a language but has planted it in us so deeply that we can talk it ourselves," Steinbeck wrote, apparently forgetting that by then

Sambo dialect had been around for well over a hundred years. As an example of Capp's "high-faluting, shimmering, gorgeous prose," Steinbeck trotted out this typical Capp passage: "After ah dances a jig wif a pig, Ah yanks out two o' mah teeth, an' presents 'em to th' bridegroom—as mementos o' the occasion!!—then—Ah really gits goin!!" And in a book-length 1970 attempt to justify the study of Al Capp, the academic Arthur Asa Berger declared: "Capp's use of an American vernacular is, in itself, an 'affront' to the social order, and has strong egalitarian implications." Only an in-

telligentsia desperate to prove that they were still down with the people could claim that mouthing minstrelsy did a democrat make.

Capp's admirers on the left warmed most of all to his savage portrayals of the big fat bad guy. In the Thirties, Forties, and Fifties, Capp reveled in drawing porcine, bejeweled tycoons and big bidnessmen with names like J. Colossal McGenius, Rockwell P. Squeezeblood, and J.P. Gorganfeller. Such caricatures, in and of themselves, were populism enough for most, and the critics duly painted Capp as a dyspeptic, chain-smoking,

wooden-legged champeen of the common man. And yet I cannot find one instance of a Capp-champion actually doing the dirty work of looking deeply into the forty-three years' worth of plodding Dogpatch storyline in order to extract evidence of the cartoonist's alleged populism. Maybe the fact that *Li'l Abner* was a comic strip, and hence popular, was sufficient.

But it's hard to blame the critics for their lackadaisical generalizations. Reading Capp's ceaseless strips is an excruciating exercise. The closest most critics came to paying attention was during Abner's famous 1948 encounter with the blobby, amorphous Shmoo. This was the episode, more than any other, that cemented Capp's reputation as a spokesman for the common man and sent the prototype cult-studs riffling through their thesauruses. Shmoos were soft little white penises, cuddly creatures with a perpetual smile and a moozikal song of "Shmoo" on their lips. They reproduced spontaneously and essentially provided everything man needed to survive, laying an endless supply of milk, aigs, and butter. When a Shmoo saw a human look at them with hunger in his eyes, the Shmoo died of happiness on the spot. The hongry Dogpatcher could then eat them broiled, so they tasted like steak, or boiled, so they tasted like chicken. Sawed lengthwise and dried, they made wood; cut in slabs, they made leather; sliced thin, they made the fahnest cloth. Abner plucked out their eyeballs to make suspender buttons and picked their meat from his grin with toothpicks made from their whiskers. If ever there was a metaphor for American abundance, the Shmoo was it. Natcherly

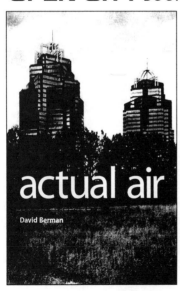

such a utopia could not stand. The swine-king of the pork industry, J. Roaringham Fatback, grew pop-eyed and indignant over the Shmoos and, in an apoplectic fit, had his double-breasted henchmen execute them all. Exactly why Fatback killed the Shmoos, nobody bothered to examine—but we will come to that later.

Almost overnight the myth of Capp's career as cornpone friend of the common man was born. Capp printed the newspaper Shmoo strips as an actual book in 1948. *The Life and Times of the Shmoo* sold seven hundred thousand copies, and on November 6, 1950, Capp, Abner, Daisy Mae, and the Shmoos made the cover of *Time* magazine. It was official: Comics were now Culture. Steinbeck's recommendation followed soon after, making comics not just pitchers but actual Writing as well. In his 1963 book, *The Politics of Hope,* Arthur Schlesinger Jr. called Capp "the most brilliant and daring of our comic strip cartoonists." Then came the ultimate compliment. In a 1965 article Capp wrote for *Life,* entitled "My Life as an Immortal Myth: How *Li'l Abner* Became the Intellectual's Delight," Capp recounted with his characteristically annoying false humility how one morning Alain Resnais, the French New Wave director, had stood humbly on Capp's doorstep and proclaimed *Li'l Abner* to be "America's one immortal myth, and the dominating artistic influence of my life." Rather than regarding this endorsement as a product of that curious Gallic tendency to see buffoons like Jerry Lewis and Mickey Rourke as avatars of a noble American savagery, Theroux presents it as proof of Capp's arteestishness. Capp himself ate up these accolades, dining and

wisecracking with the likes of Charles Chaplin, Orson Welles, and the patron saint of lifestyle liberation and bodacious ta-tas, Hugh Hefner himself. Capp even campaigned for Adlai Stevenson and John F. Kennedy. He was a celebrity, and if the liberals embraced him, then a liberal he was.

On the surface, at least. When he wasn't flying to his favorite spot in the world, London's Savoy Hotel, to have his suits tailored on Savile Row, the newly minted populist resided in his home in Cambridge—trading the yin of Yale for the yang of Harvard—and rode to work in Boston in one of his chauffeur-driven Cadillac convertibles with the name "Al Capp" painted on the door. All shows of vanity aside, Al Capp the man was in a very real sense not at all who he pretended to be. At his studio the nouveau Brahmin used a number of "assistants" to help him crank out the products of his imagination in a more efficient fashion. After the studio's morning brainstorming session Capp would rough in the action they'd concocted. Then Capp inked in the heads and bodies of the main characters—"getting the look of the strip," as Theroux puts it—and left the rest of the penciling, inking, shading, lettering, and coloring to his assistants. As is always the case in any such relationship, the people who actually did the work knew better than the bossman how to do it. Today Capp collectors pay far, far more for the *Abner* strips known to be "assisted" by Frank Frazetta, the unsung genius behind the cheesiest of Capp's oft-ogled cheesecake. (Frazetta eventually huffed out of Capp's studio and went on to great fame as the world's foremost painter of barbarians, Molly

Hatchet album covers, and big-hipped maidens in chain-mail bikinis.) The crowning touch of phoniness was this: Capp paid his assistant Harvey Curtis to sign each and every *Li'l Abner* strip with the trademark Al Capp "signature." Al Capp was not even "Al Capp."

IN THE late Sixties Capp seemed to lose interest in baiting industrialists and PR men. He had a new target now, the hippies and the student left, whom he treated with the same contempt he had always held for everyone else. Once again, Al Capp was warping and mocking a kind of white Negro—but this time it was white middle-class kids who consciously *tried* to be culturally black. First and foremost came that all-important bugaboo of the backlash, the welfare mother. Capp condensed his previous emblems of impoverished fertility, Dogpatch's Misser and Missus J.P. McFruitful and their forty-odd kids, and turned them into the decidedly more urban Miss Ann Yewly Fruitful, the national chairman of Militant Unwed Mothers (MUMs). Capp's caricature of rotund, limousine-riding businessmen (like himself) slimmed into the svelte Joanie Phonie, a thinly veiled lampoon of Joan Baez, who rode to and from her pinko charity benefits in a caviar-laden limousine. Capp tied a polky-dot tie on Abner and replaced the raggedy Dog-patchers with the equally raggedy group of barefoot student protesters he called Students Wildly Indignant about Nearly Everything (SWINE). These new underdogs made a fuss, unlike their earlier, yassuh forebears, and for that reason Capp drew them with extra venom and without the sentimentality that some had

found so endearing in the good old days.

Once again, Capp's mockery of the underdog made him a rich, rich man. Once again, the middle class leapt at the chance to embrace Capp's attack on the idle rich, but this time it was the Daughters of the American Revolution and the Elks who backed Capp. He became the prophet of the Silent Majority, fulminating against the hordes of long-haired rich kids wearing tea shades, waving placards, and hurling firebombs with their soft, pink hands. Again he made bogus populism into something of an industry: Capp stumped about college campuses on a $5,000-per-appearance lecture tour, where he wagged a nicotined finger at students and growled jowly, spittle-flecked denunciations of their hair, their "hate America" music, their privilege, their youth, and their goddamned laziness. Ever the showman, Capp even crashed John and Yoko's bed-in for peace, barging in and unleashing an incoherent torrent of abuse and invective. Capp prospered from the bitter culture wars, and he took to taking black coffee with Spiro Agnew and Richard Nixon, dining and grousing with Ross Perot and William F. Buckley Jr., and publicly threatening to run for the Senate against Ted Kennedy. Once again, Capp was a celebrity, and if the right embraced him, then a righty he was.

But by the time Capp published *The Hardhat's Bedtime Story Book* in 1972, the jig was up for him. The book was a set of dystopian essays featuring half-real, half-imagined stereotypes such as Jerry Rubin, whom Capp imagined as president of Harvbaked University in 1984—a Harvard with a Richard Speck School of Ethics and a campus Gestapo run by

Abbie Hoffman. It seemed like perfect stuff for the newly populist right, which was learning to portray itself as the ally of the average worker in his fight against a new establishment—but Capp could not get anybody to write the introduction this time. "John Steinbeck wrote the preface to my last book," Capp wrote in his own, self-described "lonely" introduction, "and in it, he nominated me for the Nobel Prize. When they gave it to him instead, it broke his heart and I vowed that never again would I cause a great man pain. And so I have not asked quite a few great men to write this preface for me."

The truth is that the right was through with Capp, and that nobody, liberal or conservative, wanted to touch Capp's book with a ten-foot pole—mainly because Capp had been trying to touch young women with *his* pole. In 1971 the *Boston Phoenix* reported that Capp had "exposed himself" and made "forceful advances" toward four separate girls in the course of one visit to the University of Alabama, and had been forced out of town by the university president. In 1972 Capp waved his cock at a married coed at the University of Wisconsin, then attempted to sodomize her. She was a "left-wing" girl, Capp said, a "do-gooder determined to remake me." She pressed charges. Capp claimed innocence but pleaded guilty to "attempted adultery," and shortly thereafter retired in disgrace. Five years later he was dead from emphysema, suffocated by his own ceaseless smoking.

But just how abrupt was Capp's conversion to the right? Take a close look at the most celebrated episode from his liberal period—the story of the Shmoo—and you will notice that the Shmoo was much more a metaphor for laissez-faire capitalism than it was for any leftist vision of utopian plenty. J. Roaringham Fatback did indeed exterminate the cute li'l creature and all humanity's hopes for easy prosperity, but not for the reason Capp's liberal-populist admirers imagined. In fact, Fatback ordered his genocide over the *protests* of his fellow bizmen, savvy capitalists who saw immediately a million new Shmoo markets that would arise for them to penetrate and exploit. "New developments don't ruin American business, Fatback!!" the Suits enthused. "They just open new fields for us!!" "Sure!" piped

up another tycoon. "Everybody's got Shmoos—plain Shmoos!! But who's got *chocolate-covered* Shmoos? There's a tremendous field, right there!!" Their ingenious list went on: salted Shmoos, canned Shmoos, candied Shmoos, Shmoo knives, Shmoo shoop—I mean soup—and so forth as the barons of business danced in an endless circle of product differentiation and brand extension. Meanwhile, the fat villain Fatback harrumphed, "I hate anything new!! . . . If those things aren't exterminated, I'll have to change my way of life—*and I hate change!!*" And so Fatback wiped out the Shmoos, subverting the true visionaries of Capp's Shmoo episode: the suit-clad seers of market-based prosperity. Fatback was a villain only because he was a lousy businessman, unable to comprehend or appreciate the eternally provident market—America's actual immortal myth.

Capp knew whereof he lampooned. In real life Al Capp was just such a seer of boundless abundance and no doubt had his share of encounters with piggish old-style businessmen. In 1948 Capp worked with the 17th Military Air Transport Squadron to airlift chocolate-filled Shmoo dolls and life-size inflatable Shmoos into Berlin—a fraction of the blessings he showered on the poor, beleaguered "common people" here at home. Capp left us Shmoo dolls, Shmoo rings, Shmoo clocks, Shmoo soaps, Shmoo banks, Shmoo salt shakers, Shmoo records, Shmoo cookie jars, Shmoo pencils, Shmoo stationery, Shmoo soda pop, Shmoo balloons, Shmoo overalls, Shmoo shampoo, and Shmoo breakfast cereal. An article about the Shmoolift in *Life* magazine rhapsodized about the "CAPPitalistic lessons" that the captive Teutonic commies might learn from the man who had invented his own prosperity.

If capitalism could just get soft and cuddly, Capp was telling us, all its—and our—problems would be solved. The metaphor even worked the other way around: Not only were Shmoos capable of becoming consumer products, but consumer products were capable of making nonbelievers into Shmoos! At one point during the Cold War Capp drew comic strip ads for Cream of Wheat in which Nogoodniks—unshaven, fanged Russian lumpkins hailing from "Lower Slobbovia"—were transformed into chirpy, white Shmoos by eating the bland, gooey stuff. "All I know about modern capitalism I learned from the Shmoo," Capp wrote in *The New Republic* in 1949. "But don't cry, kiddies, there is a real live Shmoo," he continued. "This big earth itself will give us everything we want, just as the Shmoo does, if only we'd let it alone—if only, in our passion and hatred and intolerance, we don't tear it apart."

Capp's noble way of saying, essentially, don't ever change a damn thing.

Days of Rage

One day several years ago, when I was living in Boston, I was crossing the street, and I apparently got in the way of an oncoming car. The driver was so angry that he yelled, "Get outta the way, ya fuckin' liberal!" I couldn't figure out how he drew that inference, but I was wearing a tie and had pretty long hair.

—Submitted by A. Gelman, New York City

In Readiness

A geography for your character can be learned
only after the blind cord frays. I feel impatience,
a gift perhaps, but when applied in retrospect
only a small comfort brought hence
across a footbridge, over carelessly spaced boards.
As if expecting a lamp to be lit by someone else, I await guests.
Await inexactitude. Whether or not you comply
I'll glide across the lawn in my head, away from roses planted
before we moved here or moved together at all. Herein
my reward, with grace we can settle into
as water streams down the panes and our breath condenses opposite.
In search for transport, a new cut spurns its source,
and absolution is all we need now to become complementary.
The vicinity calls out bookishness and chastises those
who have put off visiting for so long, but I like it anyway
and once again look past the rings on the table, treated
like a wing. Treats the medium like air. A deterrent unfurls
above the buildings in view, so gentle like its own breeze
so creatively laid out like all we choose among,
stark in labor, light before. Unable to generate
anything but noise we settled for thought, sorted out
whose errors were whose and added these to accumulations.
The time laid aside for further mulling has healed
into rope and twisted on itself while we idled nearby
in a game. Now that we have learned all this
an application can be sought, undone, a glistening lake.

—Beth Anderson

HANDLESS

Terri Kapsalis

I didn't want to upset him. I wanted to impress him.

He opened the car door for me. And I got in. Carefully. Gracefully. He closed the door on my hand. And I left my hand in the door.

He got in the car and we drove. Fifteen, twenty miles to dinner. He stopped the car and then he noticed.

"Your hand is in the door."

"Oh really? Why yes. Yes!" I laughed carelessly as though I had forgotten.

I never really liked my hands much anyway—stubby, not long and lean. There were short brown hairs near my knuckles in both directions. So it was not hard for me just to leave it there, leave my hand in the door. My wrist, now that is much more attractive, and without the hand it would steal attention.

I left it there, my hand. It looked strange. Lost. Sulky. But it was no longer mine and it did not concern me. When he opened the door, it fell to the ground with a thump. It looked like a glove that had seen a bad day and lay frozen and stiff from the weather.

Dinner was good. I quickly adjusted to my new handlessness. It was exciting. A challenge. How do you cut the meat, for instance. Aha! Not easy.

I didn't want to upset him. I wanted to impress him. A wrist is very handy. I could balance the fork just so, I was quite good at it actually. The wine was delicious. He is very brave.

I was starting to feel a little sad . . . from the wine, maybe. You get used to two hands. I had been raised with them. I started to feel sorry for the one in the parking lot, alone like a leftover. I considered for a moment that I could go get it, at least take it home, it would only be fair. He was talking about work.

I didn't want to upset him so I excused myself. I was sticking to the chair. This had happened before. I have a little extra in the rear. He was noticing this time that something was wrong. I wanted to impress him. I was up, but my behind was not. It sat there without me. Before he saw I spread my napkin over it like a dead soldier. No need to upset him.

In the ladies room I looked in the mirror sideways as I do—to see the tummy, the behind—none there, just a sharp drop. I am crafty. All the better to impress him. I took the scarf from my neck and tied it around my waist, pleating it here and here. And you would have never noticed.

Terri Kapsalis is a performer, health educator, and the author of *Public Privates: Performing Gynecology from Both Ends of the Speculum* (Duke University Press, 1997). She lives in Chicago.

Back at the table I let him know that I was tired of that seat (the one with my rear in it) and chose one closer to him instead. I told him I was more comfortable being closer to him. He suggested we could get even closer. I was not feeling very good, but I didn't want to upset him. He paid the bill. I had never liked my rear much. No, to be truthful it wasn't hard to part with it. When we got to the car I looked down for the last time, just to say goodbye, but it wasn't there. Dragged away or picked up or something. *Que sera sera,* I always say. And I didn't want to upset him.

We drove to his place. Very impressive. Tall. Shiny. At least fifty floors. Tasteful lamps in the lobby. Oriental carpets. Dark wood floors. He led the way down the long hall, past the security door to the el-evator. I followed and the door slid shut behind me very quickly, practically instantly. My knee was bent mid-step. The door cut through my calf like butter—as if it wasn't even there. He didn't notice, luckily. I liked those shoes.

We traveled upward for a long, long time. I used the minutes to find my new sense of balance. Quietly. Efficiently. I did not know how I would be able to get to his apartment so I leaned against his side. He took it as amour.

I moved quite skillfully, crutched on his shoulder. We reached the door to his apartment. Number fifty-two thirty-seven. I didn't know how I was going to manage once inside. But it had been a lovely evening so far. And I didn't want to upset him. I wanted to impress him.

❖ ❖ ❖ ❖ ❖ ❖

Red Terror Seizes Vegas

*T*he Venetian Resort-Hotel-Casino criticized the Culinary Workers Union Local 226 today for financing a known Communist to travel to Las Vegas in order to march with them on the Las Vegas Strip. Michele Vianello, deputy mayor of Venice and a member of the Democratic Party of the Left, was brought to Las Vegas as a part of the Culinary Union's unsuccessful campaign to thwart the success of The Venetian.

"It is unconscionable that the Culinary Union would use their members' hard-earned dollars to fly a Communist leader from Italy to Las Vegas to generate bad publicity for Las Vegas," said William Weidner, president of Las Vegas Sands Inc., the parent company of The Venetian. "Mr. Vianello's charge that one cannot recreate Venice is completely irrelevant. None of the resorts on the Strip are actually trying to recreate the cities they represent, nor are we. At The Venetian Resort-Hotel-Casino, we have created a world-class luxurious resort destination which is themed and pays tribute to the art, history, and romance of Venice. The Venetian is an asset to our tourism economy and it should not be criticized in such a superficial manner."

—Digested from Business Wire

MODERNISM AS KITSCH
Hilton Kramer's Thirty-Year Culture War

Daniel Lazare

IF YOU are one of those who dismiss the art critic Hilton Kramer as a kind of antiquated aesthete with a deep anger against the modern world and a mad glint in his prose, you should know that it wasn't always that way. Although nowadays his magazine, *The New Criterion*, specializes in Allan Bloom-style laments about leftist barbarians undermining Western culture, there was a time when he was capable of writing about high- and not-so-high-culture figures with humor, insight, and even balance. Here, for example, is how he described a 1978 Whitney Museum show devoted to the enigmatic *New Yorker* cartoonist Saul Steinberg (he of the famous "View of the World from Ninth Avenue"):

> The public that attends a Steinberg exhibition . . . does not resemble the public at other exhibitions. It moves differently and behaves differently, for it does not look as much as it reads. It also smiles a lot. Its whole manner of absorption—and there is no question about its being absorbed—is quite different from that of people looking at painting or sculpture. A Steinberg exhibition arches the back and concentrates the mind. It is an intellectual puzzle as well as a visual entertainment. It abounds in ideas. It both embraces the

world "out there" and yet obliterates it, turning everything the Steinberg mind touches into—what? A comedy of manners, certainly. But also a comedy about art and its processes of thought. . . .

This was lively and interesting, the sort of observation that makes even those of us who don't particularly care for Steinberg (such as this writer) want to keep on reading. Now consider a typical bit of late-Kramer bombast, circa 1987, in which the writer rages like a sidewalk crazy person at the leading cultural institutions of American society:

> From the lecture halls of the Harvard Law School to the glossy pages of *The New Yorker*, from the boardrooms of innumerable universities, museums, and publishing houses to the classrooms where the arts, the humanities, and the social sciences are being deconstructed and destroyed, it is the policies and doctrines bequeathed to us by the New Left in its alliance with the counterculture that determine the principle agencies and exert the dominant influence.

And if you think that's a remarkable bit of conspiracy theorizing, have a look at Kramer's, er, *unique* take on American cultural history from the vantage point of the fourth year of the Clinton administration:

> About the cultural as well as the political consequences of Stalinism, our historians are only now—thanks, in part, to the opening of the Soviet archives—beginning to tell the full story of what amounted to a massive and largely successful campaign of ideological brainwashing, conspiracy, and intimidation. . . . [A] good deal of American cultural life may be said to have been Stalinized, and at certain intervals—in the cultural life of the 1960s, for example, and with the imposition of political correctness and multiculturalism in the 1980s and 1990s—has been repeatedly re-Stalinized ever since.

Despite repeated red scares, purges, and right-wing crusades, it seems that Communism—the official Moscow variety, spelled with a capital "C"—is as powerful as ever. Although less astute observers might take certain developments, e.g., the fall of the Soviet Union in 1991, as evidence that Communism had weakened as an ideological force, Hilton Kramer, art critic, knows better.

I N A superficial sense, Hilton Kramer seems like just another member of the old *Partisan Review* circle of intellectuals who started out left and wound up moving further and further to the right in response to Sixties radicalism—some would say in response to figuring out where the money came from. The political landscape is full of such converts, ex-Stalinists, ex-Trotskyists, or ex-SDSers like Peter Collier and David Horowitz. What makes Kramer's case more interesting than most is, first, that he did it all in the name of modernism, a movement

that, at least as far as art is concerned, has always had certain vaguely anti-bourgeois connotations and, second, that he has taken aesthetic modernism much further to the right than most people would have thought possible. While some might recall the right-wing antics of T. S. Eliot, Ezra Pound, or Louis-Ferdinand Céline, in our own times it is generally assumed that the only aesthetic opinions one is likely to hear in the land of reaction are Tom Wolfe-style snipings at the New York art set with their white wine, black-on-black clothing, funny pictures, and impenetrable theoretical discourse. But Kramer reminds us that it ain't necessarily so: One can defend Picasso and even write appreciatively about Julian Schnabel and still be a card-carrying member of the loony right. How long he'll be able to keep it up, though, is another question. On one hand, there's no doubt that his presence has provided the random collection of cranks who make up the American right with a certain intellectual credibility they wouldn't otherwise enjoy. On the other hand, a man of refined sensibilities like Kramer can't help but be increasingly uncomfortable among the gun-toting, Darwin-denouncing, militia-forming know-nothings who are the constituency for the only politics Kramer now finds he can stomach. Perhaps this painful situation is what explains his increasingly wild-eyed rhetoric.

But the Hilton Kramer story is best understood as an epilogue to the remarkable 1983 study by Serge Guilbaut, *How New York Stole the Idea of Modern Art* (published, by the way, at just about the same time that *The New Criterion* was getting off the ground). Guilbaut traced the evolution of abstract expressionism from the anti-capitalism of the Thirties to a movement so mainstream that the State Department was ultimately able to make use of it in its anti-Soviet Kulturkampf. Since one of the few things everyone could agree on about action painters splattering pigment onto oversized canvases was that they had verve, then the society that produced them had to have verve as well—a syllogism that, Guilbaut showed, served the early U.S. culture warriors well. But before the State Department could utilize abstract expressionism in this manner, it had to strip it of its Depression-era radicalism. Rebellion had to be firmly separated from revolution so that it could be rendered as 100 percent American as blue jeans, bubble gum, and bebop jazz. Radicalism had to be domesticated. As the art critic Clement Greenberg, Kramer's mentor and one of the main players in this affair, put it in 1961 without the least touch of irony: "Someday it will have to be told how anti-Stalinism, which started out more or less as Trotskyism, turned into art for art's sake, and thereby cleared the way, heroically, for what was to come."

What was to come was formalism at its most hermetic, a theory which held that art could succeed as art only if left undisturbed in its own separate realm, sealed off from any and all outside forces.

This process was well under way by the time Kramer happened on the scene in the early Fifties. Born in Massachusetts to a solidly Democratic, working-class family in 1928, Kramer graduated from Syracuse University in 1950, bounced around as an English grad student for a bit, and then, after an unhappy year at Indiana University, got his first big break when Philip Rahv, one of *Partisan Review*'s two founding editors, accepted an article he had submitted on new developments in the American art scene. Such was the magazine's influence that Kramer (whose "dirty little secret" was that he had never taken an art course) became an instant authority. Offers to write poured in from *Art Digest, Commentary, The Nation*, and elsewhere. Then, in 1965, came the ultimate plum, a job offer from the *New York Times*, where he would eventually serve as cultural-news editor and chief art critic. Why did Kramer do so well? A look back at some of his early criticism suggests that it was a combination of an infectious, enthusiastic style, an air of authority (even if not totally earned), and political dependability. As Kramer was later to write, modernism by this point was enjoying an unprecedented hegemony over the art field. Its rivals—the regionalists, the social realists, etc.—had all been banished to Siberia, victims of a new orthodoxy that held that anything that was not abstract was not modern

and that anything that was not modern was not genuine art. It was an orthodoxy that Kramer not only supported but believed in—politically, intellectually, and morally.

Kramer nonetheless spent his first years in and around the *Partisan Review* carefully picking his way through the ideological mine field. While veteran *PR*-istas argued about Trotsky and the Bolshevik Revolution and Clement Greenberg struggled to hold on to some vestige of Marxism along with his ever more severe formalism, Kramer held his tongue. All the while, though, he was moving toward a class analysis of his own, one that rejected any ideological connection between the avant-garde and the left. The real connection, he was coming to think, was between the avant-garde and the bourgeoisie. For years, the two had been mortal enemies. But then a few wealthy collectors eventually broke the ice, purchasing works that had previously been despised, and rapprochement soon led to a full-scale embrace. For most critics this union of bohemia and Babbittry has been a little embarrassing, to say the least. For Kramer, though, it has carried the sort of millennial promise his colleagues once pinned on "the revolution." "Like partners in a stormy but enduring marriage," Kramer wrote in 1985, "the avant-garde and the bourgeoisie came more and more to depend on each other and even to resemble each other." One side learned how much it could shock and mock its patrons without alienating them completely, while the other learned to suffer along with their new creative-genius friends as they explored new forms of expression. Indeed, not only did the capitalist class

embrace modernism, Kramer wrote, it "created special institutions—museums and exhibition societies, schools, publications, foundations, etc.—which functioned, in effect, as agencies of a licensed opposition." The result was something new in the history of Western culture.

Kramer was no radical at this point, but neither was he the merry volcano we know today. In retrospect, the incident that seems to have pushed him over the edge was the 1964 publication of Susan Sontag's "Notes on 'Camp'" in *Partisan Review*, an essay that purported to announce a whole new way of looking at things, a new sensibility. Sontag's essay is best read as a delayed rejoinder to an equally epochal piece, "Avant-Garde and Kitsch," that Clement Greenberg published in *PR* back in 1939. Greenberg's essay had been an attempt, simultaneously ponderous and naive, to enlist high modernism in the service of socialist revolution. Kitsch, or what would later be called mass culture, was the very antithesis of real art, he argued. It served as an instrument of totalitarian control, lulling the public into complacency by assuring them that they knew what was right without having to think. Modernism, on the other hand, challenged the masses with its very difficulty. The purpose of modern art was not to declare "all power to the soviets," "down with the imperialist war," or anything else so heavy-handed, but to inspire its audience to think—to think about art, about culture and politics, about the human condition in all its aspects.

To which Sontag replied a quarter of a century later, the hell with it: If kitsch is cheap and anti-intellectual, it can also be fun, and fun is the truly revolutionary quality. "Many examples of Camp are things which, from a 'serious' point of view, are either bad art or kitsch," she declared. But so what? "The whole point of Camp is to dethrone the serious."

The essay seems to have had the same effect on Hilton Kramer that the young Bob Dylan had on Michael Harrington—one of complete shock and dismay. Kramer had *believed* when Greenberg laid down the law about modernism's moral engagement. Art was going to change the world! Yet here was Sontag celebrating kitsch precisely because it was liberated from "moral relevance." Over the years, Sontag would turn into something of an obsession of Kramer's, becoming the epitome of the self-aggrandizing literary politician he most despised. He followed the various twists and turns in her career with morbid glee. Here was Susan Sontag as the enemy of whiteness ("the white race

is the cancer of human history . . . "); Susan Sontag as the lifestyle revolutionary ("Rock, grass, better orgasms, freaky clothes, grooving on nature—really grooving on anything—unfits, maladapts a person for the American way of life"); Susan Sontag as the born-again anticommunist (readers of *Reader's Digest* "would have been better informed about the realities of Communism" than readers of *The Nation* or *New Statesman*); Susan Sontag as a latter-day Joan of Arc in war-torn Sarajevo; and, finally, Susan Sontag as laptop bombardier urging NATO to give the Serbs hell. Every time his audience's attention seemed to wander, Kramer would haul out yet another dumb Sontag quote as if to say, "See? This is what we're fighting against!"

After thirty years of official irony it's not hard to sympathize with Kramer's outrage. But Kramer just couldn't walk away from it. When Sontag went left, he

went right; when she returned to the center, he went further right still. Kramer was caught in a dilemma, as he sometimes realized in his more lucid moments. Camp was not just a new style, it was a disease, an aesthetic parasite. It needed modernism—his modernism!—in order to strike its supercilious poses. The problem, though, was that modernism seemed too old to fight it off. It was weak, enervated, "at the end of its tether," as Kramer would later write. To make matters worse, the more Kramer struggled, the more serious he became, the more he seemed to strengthen his postmodern enemies, providing them with exactly the puritanical butt their japes required. But Kramer fought on, and as he did all his ideas and his insights and his brilliance were reduced to a single point: The absolute moral authority of Art.

This was the passion of Hilton Kramer, the desperate effort to save what could not be saved. The more hopeless it became, the more frenzied his efforts grew. In his hands, Greenbergian notions of modernism as a stringently moral exercise were becoming something dangerously authoritarian. Modernism was becoming a fetish, an icon, as Kramer bowed in prayer five times a day in the direction of the Museum of Modern Art. His position became conservative in the most literal sense—he was struggling to conserve what he could of a tradition he knew to be dying.

Kramer's neocon proclivities were evident by 1970 when he lashed out at painters in New York for calling on museums to shut down temporarily to protest the invasion of Cambodia. By 1982, when he launched *The New Criterion*—"a monthly review edited by Hilton Kramer," as every cover has proclaimed since—with a half-million-dollar grant from the Olin Foundation and other such sources, they were at full boil.

The New Criterion started out cranky and ended up worse. In an opening statement, the editors quoted Sir Walter Scott (a kitsch writer if ever there was one) to the effect that the entire enterprise was motivated by outrage over "the disgusting and deleterious doctrines with which the most popular of our Reviews disgraces its pages." "Not since the 1930s," the editors went on, "have so many orthodox leftist pieties so casually insinuated themselves into both the creation and criticism of literature, and remained so immune to resistance or exposure." Within a few years, the magazine had published a neo-McCarthyite attack by the medieval historian Norman F. Cantor on the Princeton historian Lawrence Stone that was so over the top that it earned a rebuke from the neocon doyenne Gertrude Himmelfarb herself. In 1986, it published a wacky piece by Ronald Radosh asserting that a republican victory in the Spanish Civil War would have resulted in less freedom than a fascist one. (While correctly pointing out that the Soviet secret police ran riot behind Spanish republican lines, Radosh's article made one wonder why, if Franco was preferable to Stalin in Spain, Hitler would not have been preferable to Stalin in Eastern Europe.) With the publication of Allan Bloom's bestselling *Closing of the American Mind* a year later, the temperature of Kramer's writing rose even higher. He was by now seeing feminists and deconstructionists under every bed and behind every tree, united in the common project of ransacking his precious modernist canon. By 1988, he was damning an entire generation of academics to perdition because they were conspiring to ensure that art be "categorically removed from the realm of aesthetics and placed firmly in a realm where the only legitimate questions are those that can be asked about the material—which is to say, the political and economic—conditions of its production."

Loopy as this sounds, it made perfect sense in terms of Kramer's alternative universe: If art is holy, its mysteries must be defended against those who would pry too closely into the circumstances in which it is created. Faith must be secured against reason. By 1989, Kramer was calling on academia to abandon sociological analysis altogether and return to the high ground of connoisseurship, "the clear, comparative study of art objects with a view to determining their relative level of aesthetic quality." The operative word here was "relative"—Kramer was calling, in effect, for a return to the old cultural hierarchy in which artists were arranged in descending order of importance from the godlike to the semi-divine and so on.

By the mid-Nineties, *The New Criterion*'s tone had become so gloomy as to be positively Spenglerian. Thanks to the rock-loving, pizza-chomping, cigar-smoking Bill Clinton—in many ways, a figure even more distasteful to Kramer than Sontag—culture everywhere was going to wrack and ruin. "Culturally, morally the world we inhabit is increasingly a trash world," sang Roger Kimball, Kramer's tory colleague, "addicted to sensation, besieged everywhere by the cacophonous, mind-numbing din of rock music, saturated with pornography, in thrall to the lowest common denominator where questions of taste, manners, or intellectual delicacy are concerned." Kramer meanwhile took to writing a column for that well-known fount of intellectual delicacy, the *New York Post*, devoted to complaining that his former employer, the *Times*, was becoming a PC stronghold. As a member of the Adelphi University board of trustees, he got caught up in the Peter Diamandopoulos scandal when it came out that he and Adelphi's free-spending neocon president had run up a $552 bar tab one evening at university expense.

There are many ironies in this saga. The saddest and most compelling is the evolution of modernism from a movement coinciding, as Clement Greenberg once put it, "with the first bold development of scientific revolutionary thought in Europe," into something more and more associated with the authoritarian right. But another has to do with the evolution of kitsch itself. Greenberg used the term to describe art that discouraged critical inquiry and rewarded political quiescence. But this is exactly what modernism itself has become in the hands of Hilton Kramer. For him modernism is an object of worship, not a tool of experimentation; a weapon to employ against those who would probe, analyze, or otherwise demystify power. The result is not modernism versus kitsch, as it had been for Clement Greenberg, but modernism *as* kitsch.

BLIND JOZEF PRONEK AND DEAD SOULS

A. Hemon

The Red Scarf

As soon as Pronek stepped out of the plane (an exhausted steward, crumpled and hoary, beamed an "Auf Wiedersehen" at him), he realized that he had left his red wool scarf with a mustard stain from the Vienna airport café in the luggage compartment. He contemplated going back to fetch it, but the relentless piston of his fellow pilgrims pushed him through the mazy tunnel, until he saw a line of booths echoing one another, with uniformed officers lodged in them reading little passport-books, as sundry passengers waited obediently behind a thick yellow line on the floor. There was a man holding a sign with Pronek's name misspelled on it (Proniek), monitoring the throng winding between black ribbons, as if the man were choosing a person to attach the name to. Pronek walked up to him and said: "I am that person."

"Oh, you are," the man said. "Welcome to the States."

"Thank you," Pronek said. "Thank you very much."

The man led him past the passels of people clutching passports, pushing their tumescent handbags with their feet. "We don't have to wait," he said, nodding at Pronek for some reason, as if conveying a secret message. "You're our guest."

"Thank you!" Pronek said.

The man took him up to the booth filled to the glass-pane brim with a gigantic man. Had someone abruptly opened the door of his booth, his flesh would have oozed out slowly, Pronek thought, like runny dough.

"Hi, Wyatt!" said Pronek's guide.

"Hi, Virgil!" said the dough man.

"He's our guest!" said Virgil.

"How're you doin' buddy?" said the dough man. He was mustached, and suddenly Pronek realized that he resembled the fat detective with a loose tie and an unbuttoned shirt from an American TV show.

"I'm very well, sir, I thank you very much," Pronek said.

"Wha're you goin' to do here, buddy?"

"I do not know right now, sir. Travel. I think they have program for me."

"I'm sure they do," he said, flipping through Pronek's red Yugoslav passport, as if it were a gooey smut magazine. Then he grabbed a stamp and violently slammed it against a passport page and said:

A. Hemon is from Sarajevo. He currently lives in Chicago. His collection of short stories, *The Question of Bruno*, including "Blind Jozef Pronek and Dead Souls," is forthcoming from Doubleday.

"You have a hell of a time, y'hear now, buddy."

"I will, sir. Thank you very much."

What we have just seen is Jozef Pronek entering the United States of America. It

was January 26, 1992. Once he found himself on this side, he didn't feel anything different. He knew full well, however, he couldn't go back to retrieve his red scarf with the yellow mustard stain.

Virgil began explaining to Pronek how to get on the plane to Washington, D.C., but Pronek wasn't really listening, for Virgil's spectacular head suddenly became visible to him. He saw the valley of baldness between the two tufts of hair, stretching away from the emerging globe. The skin of Virgil's face was inscribed with an intricate network of blood vessels, like river systems on a map, with two crimson deltas around his nostrils. Hair was peering out of his nose, swaying almost imperceptibly, as if a couple of centipedes were stuck in his nostrils, hope-

lessly moving their little legs. Pronek didn't know what Virgil was saying, but still kept saying: "I know. I know." Then Virgil generously shook Pronek's hand and said: "We're so happy to have you here." What could Pronek say? He said: "Thank you."

He exchanged money with a listless carbuncular teenager behind a thick glass pane, and obediently sat down at a bar that invited him with a glaring neon sign: "Have a drink with us." He was reading dollar bills ("In God we trust.") when the waitress said: "They're pretty green, ahn't they? Wha' canna gechou, honey?"

"Beer," Pronek said.

"What kinda beer? This is not Russia, hun, we got all kindsa beer. We got Michelob, Milleh, Milleh Lite, Milleh Genuine Draft, Bud, Bud Light, Bud Ice. Wha'ever you want."

She brought him a Bud (Light) and asked: "What's your team in the Superbawl?"

"I don't know."

"I'm a Buffalo girl. I'm just gonna die if the Bills lose again."

"I hope they won't," he said.

"They better not," she said. "Or I be real mad."

All the TVs in the bar were on, but the images were distorted. The square heads of two toupeed men talking were winding upward like smoke, then they would straighten up, and Pronek could see them grinning at their microphones, as if they were delectable lollipops, then they would twist again. He thought, for a moment, that his eyes were not adjusted to the ways in which images were transmitted in this country. He remembered that dogs saw everything differently from people and that everything looked dim to them. Not to mention bats, which couldn't even see a thing, but flew around, bumping into telephone poles, with something like a sonar in their heads, which meant that they understood only echoes.

This is the kind of profitless thought that Pronek frequently had.

Pronek saw an elderly couple sitting down under one of the TVs. The man had wrinkles emerging, like rays, from the corners of his eyes, and a Redskins hat. The woman had puffed up hair, and she looked a lot like the Washington on the one-dollar bill. A sign behind their backs said "Smoking Section." They sat silent; their gazes, perpendicular to each other, converged over the tin ashtray in the center of the table. The waitress ("I'm Grace," she said. "How's everything?") brought them two Miller Lites, but they didn't touch them. Instead, the man took a black book out of his worn-out canvas handbag and spread it between the two sweating bottles. Then they read it together, their heads nearly touching, the man's left hand heaped upon the woman's right hand, like a frog upon a frog making love. They started weeping, squeezing each other's hands so hard that Pronek could see the woman's finger tips reddening, while her pink nails seemed to be stretching out.

This was, for Pronek, the first in the series of what we normally call culture shocks.

He roved all over the airport, imagining that it had the shape of John Kennedy's supine body, with his legs and arms outstretched, and leech-like airplanes sucking its toes and fingers. He imagined traveling through Kennedy's digestive system, swimming in a bubbling river of acid, like bacteria, and ending up in his gurgling kidney-bathroom. He stepped out of the airport through one of JFK's nostrils, in front of which there were cabs lined up like a thin mustache.

Finally, he joined the line of people trickling into the tunnel to the Washington D.C. plane. "How are you today?" said a steward, not bothering to hear the answer. Pronek had a window seat, and a man who looked as if he had just been attached to an air-compressor, like a balloon, sat next to him—the man was so fat that he occupied two seats and had to buckle his left thigh.

"Can't believe I am missing the Super Bowl," the man said and exhaled. "I went to every goddamn Redskins game this year and I had to miss the biggie. The fucking biggie. Are you a Redskins fan?"

"I'm afraid I don't even know rules of that game."

"Ah, you're a foreigner!" he triumphantly exclaimed and exhaled again. "What do you think of America? Isn't it the greatest country on earth?"

"I'm afraid I don't know yet. I just arrived."

"It's great. People are great. Freedom, all that. Best in the world," he concluded the conversation with an authoritative head twitch, and opened a book entitled *Seven Spiritual Laws of Growth*. Pronek looked out at the aluminum sternness of the wing, his body twisted, his cheek against the seat texture, whose chafing reminded him of his red scarf, and then he fell asleep, until the ascendance of his guts to his throat, as the plane was taking off, woke him up.

Marbles

Pronek hated his neck, because it always got stiff and became a knot of thick sinews. He would keep pressing

them, which would just produce more and more pain, while the sinews would wiggle under his fingers, as hard as steel cables. If he ever were to be decapitated, he thought, the executioner would be in danger, for the ax would probably bounce back and split the poor fellow's head like a watermelon. They would have to soak his neck in acid for a week or so, in order to soften the steely sinews, and then cut off his head.

Pronek and his umbrous co-passengers descended upon Washington, and he had to turn his whole body to look through the window at the feeble capital lights, "like moribund embers under the ashes of a cloudy night." (This was Pronek's thought at the moment, and we must concede it is rather nice.) The flight attendant sneaked from somewhere behind Pronek's back and startled him, shoving his face in the crevice between the fat man's chest and the seat in front of him, and asking: "Can I get you another beer, sir?" Pronek turned his whole body—the sinews resisting painfully—like a hand-puppet, toward the attendant and allowed him to provide more helpful service. The attendant seemed to be paid per smile and had the tan of an impeccably baked chicken.

Pronek was pushed into the airport building by the piston of his fellow-pilgrims, as described before.

First the gigantic tip of a nipple on a stick started flashing and hooting, then the empty carousel started revolving. Bulky bags and square suitcases began dropping out from behind the black curtain, then went—wooo!—down the slide. Pronek's faceless co-passengers swarmed around the carousel, as if they were bacteria at the bottom of a stomach, and the food to be digested was just being sent from the oral department. Pronek's bag was lost. He stared at the empty carousel, which revolved meaninglessly until it stopped and shone in conspicuous silence. Pronek had only a handbag packed with books and duty-free shop catalogs, plus a piece of three-day-old bourek, designed by his mother to sustain him on the trip, which was now—we can be sure of that—breeding all kinds of belligerent Balkan microorganisms.

Behind a frail, black, and long ribbon, there stood a man with Pronek's name (misspelled as "Pronak"), followed by a question mark. The man held it out just above his pelvis, with the lower edge cutting gently into the palms of his hands, so Pronek thought that his name had been taken away from him and given to this man, who was obviously an honest, hard-working, disciplined individual. The man shook Pronek's flaccid hand hesitantly, as if afraid that the sign might be taken away from him.

The man welcomed Pronek and asked about the trip with fake—but clearly polite—interest. "It was like Marlow's journey to see Kurtz," Pronek said. "Wow!" said the man, doubtless unaware of what Pronek was talking about—for which he shouldn't be blamed. The man had dark, short hair, retreating in disarray from his forehead, with ashen smudges behind his ears. He kindly helped Pronek inquire about the luggage, but to no avail.

Outside, it was snowing relentlessly, as if an ireful God was tearing up down pillows in the heavens. The man drove through the blindingly white maze of the blizzard. He pointed at objects and buildings, which kept popping out of the tumultuous snow like jacks-in-the-box: a gigantic toothpick, lit from below, as if kneeling worshippers were pointing flashlights at its pinnacle; a series of buildings that Pronek decided to describe in future conversations with whomever was interested in his U.S. impressions as built in a neo-Nazi, neo-classical, neo-fluffy style (which is not entirely justified, we believe).

"And this is the White House," the man said, exultantly.

"I always wandered," Pronek said, incorrectly. "Why it is called White House? Do you have to be white to live there?"

The man did not find it amusing, so he said: "No, it is because it is made of white marble."

Pronek's neck was stiffer than ever, at this point practically petrified, so he turned his whole body toward the man and put his left hand on the head recliner behind the man's nape, which shamelessly sported tufts of unruly hair. The man glanced at Pronek's hand, as if afraid that it might choke him.

"Did they use slaves to build it?"

"I don't know, but I don't believe so."

The man's name was Simon.

They drove in silence, as the storm was subsiding. By the time they got to the hotel, leafy snowflakes were butterflying, taking a break after a hard day's work. Simon complimented Pronek's English, and—having established a bond, presumably—informed him that the Redskins had won.

"I barely know rules," Pronek retorted.

"It's a great game," Simon said, and then invited him to his home in Falls Church, Virginia, to meet his wife, Gretchen, and their four daughters. Pronek readily accepted the invitation, although he knew very well that he would never see Simon again.

The hotel was a Quality Inn.

Pronek would remember—to this day—the room at the Quality Inn with eerie clarity: There was a large double bed in a green cape staring at the ceiling with its pillow-eyes; a dark TV facing the bed patiently, like a dog waiting for a treat; an ascetic chair, opening its wooden arms in invitation to a bland desk; an umbrellaed lamp, casting its light shyly on the writing surface; a heavy, matronly peach-colored curtain, behind which there was a large window with a generous vista of an endless wall. The bathroom was immaculately clean, with towels layered upon each other, resembling a snow cube. Pronek kept flushing the scintillating toilet, watching with amazement (he had an entirely

different concept of the toilet bowl than we do) how the water at the bottom was enthusiastically slurped in, only to rise, with liquid cocksureness, back to the original level. There were two rubber footprints stuck to the bottom of the bathtub and a handlebar sticking out of the wall. So Pronek cautiously let the water run, stepped onto the rubber footprints, which matched his feet exactly, and grasped the handlebar, but nothing happened.

We cannot be entirely sure what it was that he expected to happen.

He washed his pale-blue underwear and the exhausted collar of his rather unseemly flannel shirt, and then stretched them across the chair. He thrust himself upon the bed, which creaked, and lay na-

ked, trying unsuccessfully to calculate the time difference between Washington and Sarajevo (six hours), until he fell asleep.

He woke up and didn't know where he was or who he was, but then he saw his underwear spreading its pale-blue wings across the chair, providing clear evidence of his existence prior to that moment. He got up, liberated the window from the curtain's oppression, and saw that it was daytime, because some confused light clambered down the wall, and waited outside the window to be let in and scurry to the dark corners. He was delighted with the whole poetic-morning set-up, until he found out that his underwear was still moist.

He did not hear the maid because he was drying his pants with a hair-dryer, which he discovered in a holster, like a concealed revolver, by the mirror. She boldly walked in and saw him clutching his underwear with his left hand and pressing the hair-dryer's muzzle into its face, as if torturing it to confess. We should point out that he was butt-naked and was brandishing a regular morning erection. Pronek and the maid—a slim young woman with a paper tiara on her head—were locked together in a moment of helpless embarrassment, and then Pronek slowly closed the door. He sat on the toilet seat, thinking about the loss of his suitcases, which must have been freezing somewhere up in the heavens, stacked up, with all the other completely foreign and unfamiliar suitcases, in a cavernous underbelly of a plane, heading away, away from him. When he finally put on his broken-down shorts and mustered up enough audacity to face the maid, she was gone. His bed was all straightened up, and there was a piece of red heart-shaped candy on the pillow. Pronek imagined having a passionate affair with the maid, who really was a daughter of a New York billionaire, trying to lead an independent, dignified life and get on with her painting career. He could see himself moving back to New York with her; he would live in a shabby but homey apartment in Greenwich Village and support her, making love to her in saxophone slow-motion, kissing her graceful hands and dainty cheeks stained with vivid colors.

Simon waited for him at the reception desk, except that he was not Simon, but someone else who looked like Simon, save for the thick glasses and a torus of fat resting on his hips and pelvis. He serenely informed Pronek that he hoped Pronek had slept well, and that Pronek's luggage had been found in Pensacola, Florida. They drove past the same monuments and buildings, in front of which there were insectile machines, plowing away lumps of snow. They (Pronek and Simon No. 2) stopped in front of a large mansion hiding behind a marble-white set of pillars, akin to gargantuan prison bars. On the lawn, covered with whipped-creamy snow, there was a sign with an eagle spreading its awesome wings, frowning away from the house, as if angry with the inhabitants. They walked into a large hall and there was a uniformed guard under a colorful picture of the uncomfortably smirking George Bush.

"Hi, George!" said Pronek's escort.

"Hi, Doc!" said the guard, who stood with his legs spread, and his hands wedged authoritatively in his armpits. Doc disappeared into the office maze behind George's back. George ordered Pronek to wait in the hall, whose walls were covered with paintings of stuck-up men, their cheeks slightly turgid, as if their oral caverns were full of smoke they didn't dare exhale. The same angry eagle, Pronek noticed, was stretched flatly across the floor, and the ceiling was so high that "the eye struggled in vain to reach the remoter angles," to quote one of our great writers. The sign propped on a scrawny wooden stand said: "No Concealed Weapons." It was cold, so Pronek sat in an armchair, with his hands deep in his pockets, under the gaze of a man with puckered lips, and eyebrows in the shape of a distant seagull. Pronek played with marbles, which still lay in transoceanic hiatus at the bottom of his coat pockets, revolving them around each other. Then—to our surprise—a man sped out from behind George's back with his right hand extended in front of him, and a genuinely counterfeit smile. As Pronek was pulling his hand out, he said: "Welcome!" and the marbles, finally freed from their lint chains, leapt out of his pocket and began bouncing away from each other, cackling in their sudden liberty. He could still hear the echoes of the runaway marbles from distant corners, when the man asked Pronek: "So, how do you like our capital?"

"I don't know," Pronek said sheepishly. "I just arrived."

"You'll love it!" the man exclaimed. "It's great."

Apocalypse Now

IN NEW ORLEANS, Pronek stood in line, hoping to buy a real American hot dog, behind a man who had a gigantic black cowboy hat, tight denim pants and a leather belt pockmarked with silver bolts. As the man walked away, biting into his elaborate hot dog, mustard spurting out of the corners of his mouth, the excited

vendor kept looking after him: "Whoa, man! Do you know who that is? Do you know who that is? That's Garth Brooks!" The vendor had a baseball hat that was labeled "Saints" and his face had the delicate texture of a ripe pomegranate. "Who is Garth Brooks?" Pronek innocently asked. "Whoa, man! Who is Garth Brooks!? You don't know who Garth Brooks is? Whoa! He's the fuckin' greatest. You gotta be kiddin' me!" Then he addressed (to put it mildly) the next person in line, a young woman in white cowboy boots with little bells on the sides, whose blond hair was all thrust back as if she had ridden a motorcycle helmetless for a couple of hours. "That's Garth Brooks?" She shrieked and turned to the

person behind her—and a chain-reaction occurred, which propelled Pronek out of the circle of exultant exclamations. They all looked longingly after Garth Brooks, who, in trying to wipe mustard off his black suede boots, was spreading it all over them instead.

Garth Brooks, of course, is one of our finest country musicians.

IN COLUMBUS, Ohio, Pronek had dinner at the house of a blue-eyed poet who once won the John Wesley Gluppson Prize, as he was proudly informed by the host's wife. The poet and his wife, both well into their healthy sixties, were kind enough to invite a group of their valued, intellectually distinguished, friends. There was a professor of history, bow-tied, his face frosted with a sagely beard, in a tweed jacket with suede elbow patches, who was an expert on early American history, he said, in particular the Founding Fathers. "Are there Founding Mothers?" Pronek asked whimsically, but was immediately rewarded with a forgiving collective smile. There was a lawyer who once sold a script about injustice, which was never produced, but could have been directed "by Stanley Kramer himself." There was a young mousy woman with droopy eyes who had just come out of a painful, bitter divorce, and was normally a painter deeply interested in Native American spirituality. And let us not forget Pronek, the uncomfortable tourist.

They asked Pronek, who alternately picked at a piece of soy-steak and two limpid asparagus corpses, intermittently gulping red Chilean wine, the following questions:

What's the difference between Bosnia and Yugoslavia?

Huge.

Do they have television?

Yes.

Do they have asparagus there?

Yes, but no one in their right mind eats it. (Chortle on the right, chuckle on the left.)

What language do people speak there?

It's complicated.

Is the powder-keg going to explode?

Yes.

Is he going to settle in the United States?

Probably not.

Has he ever heard of Stanley Kramer?

Guess Who's Coming to Dinner?

Finally, Pronek toppled over his high wine glass, and then watched in panic, yet catatonic, as the red tide spread westward toward the woman who had just come out of a painful, bitter divorce. She yelped and said: "Blood! I had a vision of blood last night! Ah!" She pressed her temples and stared at the asparagus corpses heaped in the middle of the table. She kept pressing her temples, as if trying to squeeze her eyes out. Pronek saw her long black nails bending backwards and was afraid that they might break. She began sobbing, and everyone looked at one another, except Pronek, who looked at his supine wine glass. They sat in confounded silence; she wept, her crystal earrings rattling as her head quaked. The John Wesley Gluppson Prize winner then poured a little wine in her glass and said: "There, there now. It's a Chardonnay!" whereupon she looked at him, smiled and be-

gan wiping her tears with the tips of her fingers, whose nails were (to Pronek's relief) unbroken, with the same vigor with which she wept. Pronek said: "I am very sorry."

WHILE in Los Angeles, Pronek met John Milius, because he wrote the script for Pronek's favorite movie, *Apocalypse Now*. His office was in the building that Selznick constructed to stand in for Tara in *Gone With the Wind*—just the front part, in fact, because the building was only one room deep. Besides John Milius, who sat at his vast desk suckling a cigar as long as a walking stick, there was a man who introduced himself as Reg Buttler. He was abundantly mustached and had on a pale denim shirt, across whose chest an embroidered line zigzagged, like an EKG line. He shook Pronek's hand, and, additionally, heartily slapped his shoulder. There was a signed copy of the *Apocalypse Now* script ("From John to Reg") on the table in front of him. Pronek was allotted a large glass of bourbon and a giant cigar.

"Cuban," John Milius said. "The only good thing that communism ever produced." Reg Buttler lit Pronek's cigar, which kept wiggling, too large to handle, between his feeble fingers.

Then Reg Buttler put his right ankle on his left knee, and pulled the leg violently towards his pelvis, apparently trying to break his own hip. The sharp tip of Reg's elaborately engraved cowboy boot was directly pointed at John Milius, and Pronek thought that if he had a secret weapon in that boot—something that would eject poisonous pellets, for instance—he could kill John Milius in an instant.

"Do you people in Sarajevo like Sam Peckinpah?" Milius asked.

"We do," Pronek said.

"No one made blood so beautiful as old Sam did," Milius said.

"I know," Pronek said.

"I didn't know you could watch American movies there," Reg Buttler said.

"We could."

"So what's gonna happen there?" Milius asked.

"I don't know," Pronek said.

"Thousands of years of hatred," Reg Buttler said and shook his head compassionately. "I can't understand a damn thing."

Pronek didn't know what to say.

"Hell, I'll call General Schwarzkopf to see what we can do there. Maybe we can go there and kick some ass," Milius said.

"Like we kicked Saddam's ass," said Reg Buttler. "Damn, that was fuckin' good. We kicked that bastard's ass."

"General Schwarzkopf told me," Milius said, "that the Marines were the best. Those boys are the best."

Pronek inhaled too much cigar smoke, so he abruptly coughed and spurted bourbon on the *Apocalypse Now* script, while a rivulet of snot ran down to his chin.

"War brings out the best and the worst in people," Milius said. "And only the fittest survive."

Pronek took out his hanky and wiped his nose, his chin and *Apocalypse Now*, respectively. Reg looked determinedly to the right, then to the left, clearly mulling over a profound thought.

"Do you want to stay in this country?" Milius asked Pronek.

"You should," Reg Buttler said. "It's a damn good country."

"I don't know," Pronek said.

"I'll call General Schwarzkopf and see what we can do about it. Listen, if you have nothing to do tomorrow, we can go out to the shooting range and raise some hell."

"I'm there with ya!" Reg Buttler said.

But Pronek had a meeting that he couldn't miss (which we know was not true) so he politely declined. Before he left, he had a picture taken in front of the building that used to act as Tara. There he is—our foreign friend—teeny with the house in the background, sturdy pillars all lined up behind, like cousins in a family picture, lawns glaring green. He is standing a foot away from Reg and Milius. Milius's hand is resting on Reg's shoulder, the two of them like Scarlett O'Hara and her pop, except there is no fake, painted, blood-red sunset, against which they could appear to be shadows, as the music reaches an orgasmic pitch.

Powerslave

Large crowds gather in late industrial style:
Austin, MN; Peoria, IL; Flint, MI.
Quantrill's corporate raiders and John Brown's ghost.
DNA marketplace and love for sale, love on the rocks.
Starting a new life on her father's South Dakota farm.
Sallow August afternoons, while ADM undercuts
small-scale production.

Diesel trucks idle outside a Flying J travel plaza.
A cardboard sign held out back reads in large black marker:
"Trying to get home to see my sweetheart."
A baby on the way and two already sleeping
in the parents' small room. Generations
of atmospheric pressure, of violence,
spoken in sharp words.
Hunting frogs at night with a lantern and stick.

Illusory nomad ego raids on the culture.
Critique. The non-metaphysical: a rescued poverty.
The danger of replacing ethics with aesthetics.
You make me tense. *What a life a mess can be.*
History from below and a barter economy,
like trading braiding for baby-sitting.
A documentary urge and language to chew.

—Alan Gilbert

BIRCHISMO

DAN KELLY

We'll teach you how to spot 'em
In the cities or the sticks,
For even Jasper Junction is just full of Bolsheviks
The CIA's subversive, and so's the FCC
There's no one left but we and thee
And we're not sure of thee.
                    —*"The John Birch Society," by The Chad Mitchell Trio*

SOMEWHERE in the green blankness of southern Michigan, just off Highway 94, stands a lonely little sign declaring "Get US Out of the UN!" If you're paying attention to the road you'll miss it, but trust me, it's there. I first noticed the sign on the way from Grand Haven to Chicago a few summers ago, and as a rubbernecking spectator of fringe political thought, I assumed it was the work of a local militia or perhaps even a cell of cantankerous Constitutionalists, afeared the New World Order was encroaching on the sovereignty of New Buffalo, Michigan. Filing it away in my memory jar, I planned to uncover the sign's mysterious origins at another time.

Two years passed, and while visiting a gun show in Grayslake, Illinois, my question was answered. There as much to collect kook literature as to peruse Glocks and SKS rifles, I came across a gentleman in red flannel selling books, videos, and pamphlets, each pushing various fringe-dweller hot buttons. Topics ran from the dreaded New World Order to Her Satanic Majesty President Hillary to, hello, the United Nations, which we had to get US out of, pronto. I was mildly surprised to discover the source of this particular enthusiasm, the same one I had noticed in Michigan's black-stripe wilderness: the John Birch Society. I had discovered a dinosaur bone in my own backyard—the bone, though, was still connected to a reasonably lively dinosaur.

If your first reaction to the phrase "The John Birch Society" is a bewildered "Whoozat?", it's a telling sign of your youth. The John Birch Society was, is, and ever shall be the world's most stringently anticommunist organization, dedicated to finding, exposing, and squashing out every aspect of the global Communist conspiracy. The group was founded in

This is Dan Kelly's second article for THE BAFFLER. He was the editor of *Chum* magazine, and his work has been published by Loompanics Unlimited, Feral House, and *The Nose*. He lives in Chicago.

1958 by retired candymaker Robert H. W. Welch, who, rather than playing checkers or wandering the beach with a metal detector, chose to spend his golden years assembling a cabal of industrialists and declaring holy war on Marxism. Welch had grand plans for his little society. Star-chamber visions filling his head, Welch imagined a titanic secret organization that would checkmate the ever more secretive Communists' every move.

The John Birch Society's heyday came during the early Sixties. While many recall that decade as an age of butt-naked radicalism with a Jefferson Airplane soundtrack, the Sixties were also the salad days of the far right. Culture-shocked average folk desperately sought a way out of the oncoming sybaritic morass, and Welch was only too happy to give directions: Take an extreme right and drive on forever.

As for John Birch, we'll never know what he would have thought of his eponymous society. Unlike Horst Wessel or Nathan Hale, he never joined the club that would have him as a martyr. A young Bible-banging missionary from backwoods Georgia, Birch relocated to China in the Forties to evangelize the heathen Chinee. When the United States entered World War II, Birch rearranged his career plans, enlisted in the Army, and quickly rose to the rank of captain. After several years of pushing Jesus, performing OSS intelligence work, and earning a chestful of medals, the twenty-seven-year-old Birch was nabbed by the Red Chinese and executed a scant nine days after the end of the war. In all probability, Cap'n Birch might have slipped between history's cracks had Welch not learned of his plight in the files of the Senate Internal Security Subcommittee.

According to contemporary accounts, John Birch was a decent enough fellow, albeit one whose sphincter never knew the meaning of the words "at ease." But in Robert H. W. Welch's approximation, Birch was much more. To hear Welch tell it, Birch was an amalgam of Jimmy Stewart and John Wayne, with a jigger of James Bond to boot. As a martyr he was ideal—a clean-cut, God-fearing, good-looking kid, cut down in his prime by pinko scum. Indeed, for Welch he was nothing less than the first casualty of the nascent Cold War.

As for Welch, he was born to do battle on the home front. As Birch literature proudly recounts, the candyman was something of a child prodigy. Born in 1899 and home-schooled, not surprisingly, he entered the University of North Carolina at the age of twelve. In 1917 he moved on to the U.S. Naval Academy, and in the following year to Harvard Law School where, according to society literature, "his stubborn mind vexed his liberal pro-fessors." Their vexations soon ceased, though, as Welch dropped out in 1920—strangely, at the top of his class. Welch proceeded to enter the family business, applying his "stubborn mind" to vice presidential duties at the Welch Candy Company and inventing Sugar Babies along the way. (Welch was outdone, however, by his brother James, who was both company president and creator of the more popular Junior Mints.) Not coincidentally, JBS charter members were men very like Welch—cronies from his big business days, retired from years of over-seeing production and managing underlings, now eager to apply their knowledge to this great land of ours.

Welch was, naturally, an avid reader of Spengler's *Decline of the West,* from which he deduced the idea that the Old World was sliding into the dotage of collectivism, and if America was to avoid the same fate it had to reactivate George Washington's isolationist policies. The literatus who gave the Birch Society its paranoiac frisson, however, was Nesta Webster, a high-born British lady who wrote several standbys of the conspiracy theorist's library. Webster spent her life exposing the intricate web betwixt the Bavarian Illuminati, Jews, Communists, and all those in between in such tomes as *Secret Societies and Subversive Movements* and *The World Revolution.* Inspired by Mme. Webster, Welch became convinced that the Illuminati—supposedly founded in 1776 to bring "illuminated" individuals together to solve all the world's woes—survived to the present day as ghosts in the global machine, pulling the levers and causing the historical events we hoi polloi assume to be accidental.[†] Welch's stroke of genius was to extrapolate that the Illuminati's ultimate goal was to create a one-world socialist government. Communism was their most devastating weapon, its enervating influence sucking the life from a nation and converting its population into a huddled mass of hollow men.

Add to all this conjecture the all-too-real cabals of high-ranking government

---

[†] Webster's most prominent recent disciple is none other than the Rev. Pat Robertson, whose 1991 book, *The New World Order,* relies heavily on her anti-Semitic hallucinations.

officials and plutocrats who *do* meet periodically to tug at the world's puppet strings, and who were ecstatically celebrated in historian Carroll Quigley's 1966 book, *Tragedy and Hope*. The Illuminati may have been a projection of Welch's imagination, but the Council on Foreign Relations, founded in 1920, David Rockefeller's Trilateral Commission, founded in the early Seventies, and the ultra-spooky Bilderberg Group are all very real, and have corporate presidents, media kings, and financial czars at their helms. Quigley, of course, thought all this was just jake, as the industrialists, world leaders, et cetera were no doubt coming together for the good of humankind.

Welch saw things differently. Such stuff was not only dangerous, it was an outright offense to American sovereignty, the Constitution, apple pie, proper flag-folding technique, and all else Welch held dear. Outrageous though it seemed, the Birch Society's obsession with conspiracy ran deep in the American grain, arising directly from the widespread nineteenth-century belief that secret societies were antithetical to democracy. Welch saw the shadow government's imprint everywhere, and in keeping with his own era's notions of the Republic's enemies, he simply recast Communists in the villain's role, rather than the traditional Masons, Jesuits, or Jews. His small-government politics were equally unremarkable. The society's motto could easily have been the credo of some state Republican Party: "Less government, more responsibility, and—with God's help—a better world."

Despite their admirably homegrown paranoia, the Birchers were nevertheless considered a trifle dotty. Every reformer has his critics, but Robert Welch kept providing his with devastating ammunition. Welch's first book, *May God Forgive Us* (1952), started the wrecking ball swinging with its revelation that rather than fighting Communism like they were supposed to do, our government had actually been aiding and abetting the Red Menace. Joe McCarthy, predictably canonized by the Birchers, was right all along. The "loss" of half of Europe and all of China was the work of high-level pinks in the U.S. government—with a special commendation awarded to Truman administration secretary of state/evil genius Dean Acheson.

What really tattooed Welch and the society with oddball status forevermore, though, was his declaration that President Dwight D. Eisenhower was a card-carrying Leninist. In the early years of his crusade Welch penned a long letter to selected friends outlining Eisenhower's alleged side-job as a puppet of his Soviet masters. Welch closely examined Ike's military career, describing his every move as yet another tactic to gain precious postwar ground for the occupying Reds. In 1963 the letter became a book, *The Politician*, and in the public's mind it established Welch's reputation as a cast-iron kook.

Today the thought of dubbing Ike a pinko seems merely strange, but back then it had an air of treason about it. While America was not exactly ready to roll in the hay with the Soviets, people were equally reluctant to wallow once again in the McCarthyist mud. Welch had no such scruples. In *The Politician*, FDR, Truman, both Dulles brothers, and favorite Birch Society punching bag Chief

Justice Earl Warren were all said to be witting agents of The Conspiracy, ready to roger Lady Liberty at the snap of Moscow's fingers.

In that same vein, the Birchers also favored Tailgunner Joe's love of authoritative-sounding yet unverifiable statistics. The Communist takeover, for example, could be monitored like a weather report. Communist control of the United States measured at 20 to 40 percent in 1958, rising to 30 to 50 percent in 1959, and topping out at a sizzling 40 to 60 percent in 1960. In fact, in the Birchers' estimation almost everyone was in on The Conspiracy. NATO, for example, was the first step in signing over America's soul and sovereignty. Equally demonic were the World Health Organization and UNICEF, which funneled "charitable" funds into the maleficent United Nations.

And the list rolled on. Birch targets included the Social Security system, the Federal Reserve, income tax, welfare, foreign aid of any sort, urban renewal, the AMA, compulsory integration, the civil rights movement, and the brain-bending practice of water fluoridation (cf., General Jack D. Ripper in Stanley Kubrick's *Dr. Strangelove*). Even defense spending was in doubt since Birchers believed that the real Communist threat arose from within. If that wasn't terrifying enough, almost all America's universities, corporations, foundations, more than seven thousand of its clergymen, and a guesstimated 60 percent-and-rising segment of the mass media were rife with hardcore Communists, fellow travelers, and "Comsymps" (a word coined by Welch for those he could not directly accuse of being Communists). Our once great nation now glowed pinker than Pepto Bismol. Welch admonished his troops in no uncertain terms, "Get to work, or learn to talk Russian."

Many contemporary conservatives, such as McCarthy revisionist Richard Gid Powers, try to pass off the Birch Society as something of a liberal invention, a particularly lunatic bit of fringe on which the media focused in order to discredit the worthy cause of anticommunism. But the Birchers were far more than that. For all its Chicken Little paranoia, the JBS popularized the strategy that the right would employ so ably for the next three decades: unremitting war on the snobbish, effete intellectual elite—a gang the neoconservatives soon learned to call by their correct name, "the New Class," rather than the more inflammatory "Communists."

Not surprisingly, before Welch turned on his weird idea faucet, the right was happy to welcome the JBS on board. The Birch Society not only brought together the usual GOP constituents—"wealthy businessmen, retired military officers, and little old ladies in tennis shoes," in the words of one contemporary observer— but also attracted a fair number of young people, who appear in photos of Bircher meetings dressed in sensible suits and flower print dresses.

Nonetheless, the cracks in Welch's ideological pot continued to spread. Supercilious superconservative William F. Buckley Jr. took some whacks at Welch in his *National Review*, though he was careful not to offend the society's membership at large. Buckley and Co. sensed a change in the political winds, and no doubt appreciated the Birchers' potential appeal to the average Joe. Now if only . . . if only the head of the beast could be hacked off, and replaced with someone more, well, sane.

Fat chance. Robert Welch was the JBS, and the JBS was him. And though Bob had all the charisma of a dish of warm flan, he nevertheless managed to instill a startling zealotry in his followers. If Welch was a Hitler, as his lefty critics charged, he was a Führer on Thorazine, his arms bound to his sides to prevent potentially electrifying gesticulations. Despite this, Welch's self-made superpatriot status was believable to some. He inspired elements of the Silent Majority to speak up more than any (other) pompous Ivy League ass ever could.

What was most frightening/inspiring about the Birch Society was that, despite its flaky reputation, it worked. It was an ideological juggernaut, structured like a corporation, and filled with dues-paying members who were that rarity in Sixties American politics: right-wing activists. One contributor to the 1964 anthology *The Radical Right* estimated that, at its peak, the JBS had more than four thousand chapters and a hundred thousand dues-paying members. (Exact figures are unattainable, as society membership lists have always been classified.)

Mass-mediated memories of the Sixties always give prominence to the SDS, the Yippies, and other left-wing organizers and protesters, but the Birchers were out there too, banging on doors, organizing protests, and writing to their congressmen. And that wasn't all they did. As it turned out, the Birchers weren't playing by Dale Carnegie's rules.

Welch once said, "It is one of our sorrows that, in fighting the evil forces which now threaten our civilization, for us to be too civilized is unquestionably to be defeated." The answer, then, when fighting Communism, was to use Communism's tactics. Like an underground army of Hugh Beaumonts, the Birchers collectively heard and obeyed. Through his monthly *Bulletins*, Welch taught his local chapters the finer points of fifth column activity. In order to better oversee the proper dispensation of education to America's youth, members were advised to seize control of their local PTA. Members were also to infiltrate groups suspected of having socialist leanings and to attend and disrupt "pro-Communist" gatherings—which could mean anything from heckling a professor at a nearby university to protesting a Russian art exhibit. Also, as the JBS's popularity began to wane, the head Bircher set up front groups and ad-hoc committees to lure those who wouldn't be caught dead at a Birch Society cell meeting. Such fronts included the well-known Committee to Impeach Earl Warren, the innocuous-sounding Freedom Club, the Realtors for American Freedom, and the double-dutch mouthfuls of the Committee Against Educating Traitors at Government Expense and the Committee to Warn of the Arrival of Communist Merchandise on the Local Business Scene. It was often possible for an everyday citizen to attend a Birch meeting without realizing it.

Birchers also took it upon themselves to flood newspapers, radio, and television stations, and local, state, and national government offices with barrages of letters and phone calls, whenever one or the other dared to act in opposition to Birch philosophy. Other psychological blitzkriegs literally brought the war home to the Birchers' perceived enemies. Repeated anonymous late-night phone calls; false fire alarms; embarrassing and annoying classified ads featuring the mark's home address—these and other "I didn't order these pizzas"-level pranks filled the Birchers' black bags.

Despite all this fiercely patriotic activity, the Birchers' days were numbered. Whether it was by an ingenious Masonic plot, or simply enough decent folks growing tired of the Birchers' bullshit, the inevitable karmic backlash occurred.

Owing to their unequivocal views and quasi-fascistic structure, the Birchers were often, at times lazily, lumped in with the likes of the Klan, the neo-Nazis, and the more reactionary militias. No surprises there: As a superpatriotic organization, the JBS was a freak magnet. As fast as Welch and a handful of conscientious chapter leaders kicked out the bigots filling their ranks, more joined up—promoting their poison behind Welch's back, and often right under his nose. The bigot label left its mark. The JBS became viewed as a gateway drug to the harder stuff.

Charges of anti-Semitism kept cropping up. Welch himself wasn't an anti-Semite—even the Anti-Defamation League grudgingly acceded to that fact—and the JBS, while not a model of strength through diversity, was established to discriminate against commies and commies alone. In the lower ranks, on the other hand, those of anti-Semitic inclination cut society literature with racist classics like William Guy Carr's *Pawns in the Game* and American Nazi Party ephemera. The JBS ideology of US versus the Insiders was equally worrisome. Use of such Bircher buzzwords as "Illuminati," "Insiders," and "Internationalists" as euphemisms for "Jews," "Jews," and "Jews," respectively, was not unheard of. Welch may not have been an anti-Semite, but his apparent naiveté about the sources of his theories was hard to swallow. In his book *Birchism Was My Business*, Gerald

Schomp, a former chapter leader, recounted that Welch was one day seized by the bright idea of rounding up as many right-wing Jews as possible (no easy trick, according to Schomp) and creating yet another front group: the Jewish Society of Americanists.

The Birchers' pro-cop tack—"Support Your Local Police" is undoubtedly their best-known slogan—also spooked many non-cop Americans. Cops gravitated to Birchism like hippies to hash, enticed by the JBS's pooh-poohing of civilian review boards, whose presence would have had a chilling effect on the thin blue line's God-given right to crack skulls. JBS cells sprang up in police departments from coast to coast. Regional manager Thomas J. Davis proudly trumpeted the presence of one hundred Birchers on the NYPD payroll in 1964. In Santa Ana, California, a cell of twenty to thirty Birchers in blue waged a campaign to oust their chief and replace him with one of their own. Support them? Who could get close enough?

THESE days, the lot of the professional paranoid grows ever more difficult. The world has lost both Robert Welch (he died in 1985) and the Soviet Union. New times call for new ideas, especially about who "THEY" are, and how best "THEY" can be combated.

Fortunately, Welch discovered a new world of revelations well in time for the end of the Cold War. It dawned on him that he had it backwards all along: It was the UN that ran the Soviet Union, not vice versa. Forget learning Russian; it's Esperanto that we'll have to study unless we are willing to disrupt UN preparations to overrun our streets, seize our homes, violate our womenfolk, and use the Constitution as toilet paper. This new apocalypse even has a name, found beneath that freakish "pyramidclops" on the back of every dollar bill: "Novus Ordo Seclorum," the New World Order invoked by both Presidents Nixon and Bush.

To give the devil his due, the modern JBS still advocates education over insurrection, even in this age of militias and ATF showdowns. Furthermore, Birchers are not flying saucer, cattle mutilation, and hollow earth theorists—they deal only in the implausible, not the improbable. Surprisingly, they even oppose organized militias, believing that the Second Amendment's reference to a "well-regulated militia" permits firearm ownership but does not give free rein to form private armies. After all, unrestrained extremism frightens the average schmucks, putting more power into Janet Reno's claws and allowing Clinton to dispense freedom-trammeling laws like a gumball machine.

Allowing cooler heads to prevail hasn't necessarily swelled the JBS's ranks. In comparison with what it once was, the JBS undoubtedly suffers these days from a severe dearth of manpower. Of the alleged hundred thousand members of the Sixties, only eighty thousand or less remained in the Seventies, leading to an even more dramatic depopulation during the Reagan years, according to some sources. An e-mail request to the society for a current head-count was met with claims of confidentiality—rarely a sign of a boisterously healthy organization.

Ah, but while Birch numbers are small, the hardest of cores remains. Like the red-flannelled gentleman at the gun show, today's Birchers are a passionate lot, driven to expose what their literature now describes as a "satanic Conspiracy." Over six hundred thousand copies of the "Conspiracy" issue of the JBS house organ, *The New American,* were hawked by loyal Birchers in 1997—both independently and through the society's American Opinion bookstores. Passion is definitely a prerequisite for JBS membership. Even with the not-smallish membership fee of $48 a year (lifetime memberships have soared from the $1,000 bargain rate of the early Sixties to $2,000 today), one is entitled to little more than a subscription to the JBS *Bulletin,* regular chapter meetings, and a clean conscience, I suppose.

Thirty-nine dollars arranges for delivery of the thin,

four-color *New American,* which emanates from Appleton, Wisconsin, a town significant only as the hometown and current receptacle of Saint Joe McCarthy. To read the magazine is to realize how almost mainstream the Birchers have become—due more to the nation's successive listings to the right since 1968, of course (*The New American*'s Web site carries a ringing endorsement from Pat Buchanan) than any behavior modification on the JBS's part.

The New American dedicates itself to providing those "facts and perspectives omitted from other national media," as they put it, including, in recent issues, a detailed nine thousand-word story on the august nobility of Pinochet and the infamy of that former despot's present persecution by "the global elite"; a complaint about "gynecological probing" in the public schools; reach-for-your-revolver headlines like "Christian Slaves Freed, UN Objects," and "UN Wants to Tax E-mail"; an essay comparing and contrasting our nefarious Chief Executive with fugitive hippie murderer Ira Einhorn; and, of course, the latest dispatches from the ongoing war over water fluoridation.

Naturally, the truly educated Bircher should also partake of the society's breathtaking array of ultraconservative publications and videos. "The Robert Welch Presentations," for example, once available only in 8 millimeter film format, have been collected into eight hours of videotape, with the putty-nosed Welch shuffling papers and clamoring about "the principles of proper government and the conspiratorial influence in the twentieth century." Once $130, the Tao of Welch can now be yours for just eighty bucks. Books peddled by the JBS include *Disney: The Mouse Betrayed,* which exposes "pedophile and sex abuser problems at Disney World" and "how Disney's Hollywood Records produces some of the most violent, pro-suicide, and pro-Satan music in the industry."

Historically, the Birchers have had little luck in getting their own into public office. Most Birchers with any real political experience joined after leaving office, as in the case of one-term congressman Howard Buffett, father of billionaire investor Warren Buffett. Similarly, those politicians who, unmindful of the effects of political poison, proudly declared their JBS membership—as did California Republican Representatives John H. Rousselot and Edgar Hiestand in 1962—often found themselves promptly ousted by the voters. They didn't have far to fall. Most former Bircher politicos easily "transitioned" to positions within the JBS. How many Birchers held legislative power in the Sixties will probably never be known. In 1961, however, conservative paladin Barry Goldwater stated that a search for Birchers through the hallowed halls of the Capitol Building "would turn up a lot of embarrassed people." The last noteworthy and open member of the JBS to hold national elected office—the society's chairman, no less—was Representative Larry McDonald of Georgia back in the early Eighties. McDonald also made the unfortunate decision to board KAL 007, the passenger plane shot down by the Soviets in 1983, undoubtedly sending the Birchers into paroxysms of shivering paranoia.

With the recent flowering of the right, though, one hardly has to be a JBS member to support the society's once-kooky beliefs. Representative Ron Paul, a former Libertarian candidate for president and a major proponent of taxpayers' rights (namely the right to pay few or none), has proposed measures to withdraw U.S. membership and funding from the United Nations. A particular sweetheart of the Birch fraternity is the notorious Representative Helen Chenoweth of Idaho, who finds time in her busy schedule to write for *The New American*. "Thank goodness for those, such as the John Birch Society," gushes Congressman Chenoweth (as she insists on being addressed), "who are unashamed to advocate love of country, defense of nation, and an abiding commitment to our Constitution."

As for potential future Birchers, today's JBS has had better luck getting in touch with the kids than Bob Welch ever did. One pet project is Robert Welch University, which, the Good Lord willing, will soon become a fully functioning, four-year liberal arts college, empowered to issue degrees in God-fearing 100 percent Americanism. As it stands now, though, Robert Welch University exists only in the form of a thirty-thousand-volume library, every last damn book of which deals with the "preservation of our heritage of freedom." One particularly fun aspect of the JBS is the summer camp held under the Bob Welch U. banner. While the typical activities of volleyball, canoeing, hiking, and singings of "Kumbaya" are practiced, campers can also take classes designed to remediate the bum education they pick up at Illuminati-run public and private schools: "Our Godly Heritage," "What is Humanism?", "Global Tyranny—The UN," "The Life of John Birch," and, as an alternative to making wallets and weaving lanyards, "Salesmanship." Other activities include the "Night

Patrol," wherein camp counselors brandishing swords and funny hats mount raids on the campers' cabins at random hours, teaching them the hard-learned value of hating secret police. Parents can also be assured that no funny business takes place between campers of opposite, or even the same, sexes. Counselors oversee the campers' activities twenty-four hours a day. What was that about oppressive governmental control?

Today's respectable conservatives, looking down from their amply funded think tank posts, find it convenient to cry boo to the John Birch Society, dismissing it as a political curiosity for which they claim neither affinity nor responsibility. Yet, for the past thirty years, these same right-thinkers have fueled their successful reconquest of government with a blaring populism that bears a red-haired milkman's resemblance to the wacky faiths of the JBS. Silent, righteous majorities rising against a hated liberal elite; defiantly normal Americans versus a sneaking, manipulative "New Class" of journalists, professors, bureaucrats, and social workers (humanistic sodomites, one and all): However contemporary conservative thinkers might protest, this is a strategy for which they owe the John Birch Society a debt of gratitude. Welch and company converted the McCarthyite witch-hunt into something more universal: a culture war between God's patriots and an international, octopod cabal of quivering Great Society Clintonistas.

While it is true that the contemporary right takes great pains to keep talk of The Conspiracy far from its public presentations, and while it is also true that the Birchers hold no truck with the likes of Gingrich or the Bushes (globalists all), their weird theorizing is a historical bridge between the Joe McCarthy sideshow and the more successful populism of Irving Kristol and the neoconservatism of David Horowitz.

Most crucially, the Birch Society was among the first to crystallize and capitalize on that most compelling of rightwing faiths: the feeling, shared by so many of the nation's privileged and powerful, that they are, in fact, the persecuted ones, the ones whose towers are forever in danger of being toppled. Welch's true accomplishment was calling together into a protest movement a generation of strutting, financially solvent, middle-aged Americans, fresh from bombing the hell out of Dresden and Hiroshima, and still intoxicated with their new role as the first superpower; a generation for whom the landmark events of the Sixties were an unpleasant series of pimp-slaps. Welch did more than he could ever know to prove his hero Spengler's theories, beckoning his followers into a uniquely American brand of collectivism.

Going for the Gold

*P*eter Vidmar, premier male gymnast for the United States at the 1984 Olympics and a well-known motivator of America's top corporations and associations, will describe the requirements for "The Perfect 10" using the ROV (risk, originality, virtuosity) principles and corresponding pommel horse demonstrations to motivate, uplift, and entertain.

—From a brochure for the International Association for Financial Planning's "Success Forum '99"

PARADISE SHOT TO HELL

The Westbrook Pegler Story

J. C. Sharlet

WHAT kind of times do we live in when syndicated radio host G. Gordon Liddy can "neutrally" remind listeners to shoot for the head when targeting federal agents? Times pretty similar to the heyday of Westbrook Pegler, the It Boy of attack journalism, now a tragic and largely forgotten figure. "The angry man of the press," as he was known in his midcentury prime, Pegler was one of the most widely read newspaper columnists in the country. From the Depression through the Cold War he tilted at suspects familiar to Rush Limbaugh's fans: foreign subversives, swindling politicians, the First Lady, corrupt union bosses, the elite, the effete, and, of course, homosexuals. For guys like Pegler and Liddy, These Days are always understood to be After the Fall: This used to be a damn good country until "they" made a hash of it.

Pegler wielded his well-sharpened prose like a knife in a street fight. He was the kind of writer who could cheer on a lynch mob (as he actually did in 1936; he sincerely believed the victims had it coming) or exhort solid citizens to join strikebreakers "in the praiseworthy pastime of batting the brains out of pickets." In his lighter moods, Pegler refined his homophobic invective on minor targets such as the literary critic Clifton Fadiman—"the bull butterfly of the literary teas"—and then, more encouraged by the wounds such words inflicted than any particular dislike for homosexuality, he turned his anti-gay guns on bigger game, "outing" Woodrow Wilson and Frank Sinatra. (When Sinatra sought out Pegler to give him a beating, the singer brought Orson Welles as a witness. Pegler made a getaway, but he retaliated in print by praising Welles as a "dear, roguish boy [whose] whole nature seems to chitter and cheep in the language of the elves.")

Light moods were uncharacteristic of Pegler, though; more often he aimed to maim, even to kill. He channeled hatred so pure that more than one colleague blamed the death of Heywood Broun, his liberal contemporary and ex-friend, on a column in which Pegler named Broun a liar. And Broun got off easy. In 1965 Pegler wished of Robert Kennedy that "some white patriot of the Southern tier will spatter his spoonful of brains in public premises before the snow flies." By the time he called the hit on RFK, Pegler had declined into unhinged dotage, bitter and

J. C. Sharlet is a newspaperman in Washington, D.C.

banished from respectable journalism by his own cussedness, and quickly alienating even his friends on the far right with his unabashed anti-Semitism.

So what would prompt an old lefty like Murray Kempton to write, upon Pegler's departure from the mainstream press in 1962, that "he goes with honor as he has lived with honor," and that "he was true to us at the end, truer than we are to ourselves"?

Perhaps Kempton was feeling nostalgic for what was even then a dying breed of journalist: the tradesman, the uneducated skeptic, the worker whose product was prose. In his prime Pegler was that and more: He understood his job as a kind of combat, and he recognized his enemies as power and authority. Unlike Limbaugh, a self-styled entertainer who wouldn't dream of biting the hand that feeds him, Pegler not only bayed at the amorphous, alien forces of moral disorder, but often enough turned on his masters themselves. That's why Pegler is worth recalling even now—not for the substance of his anger, but for its quality, the rage that drove him to swing again and again at anyone he thought had it in for the common man.

Pegler's common man was the beleaguered man in the middle, getting it from both sides. His columns plied a deluded nostalgia for a golden age of small-r republicanism he believed had passed in America, a time when every man made his own way, when "government" meant the military, and pampered rich men were a European disgrace. So Pegler bellowed to throw out the crooked union bosses, and the unions too; throw out the politicians and the tax men and the luxuries their collections paid for; throw out the immigrants; throw out the New Deal and bring back the Old, and the golden age would be ours again. In 1938 Pegler elaborated this notion on the front page of the *New York World-Telegram*, where his column occupied the space usually reserved for breaking news stories. In a rant titled "Those Were the Days" (curiously presaging the theme song of Norman Lear's *All in the Family*) Pegler demanded, "Next time Mr. Roosevelt or Honest Hal Ickes, the House Dick of the New Deal . . . or any of those honorary proletarians who swing towels in that corner of the ring sound off in disrespect of the Old Deal I would appreciate it if somebody would refresh my memory on just what was wrong with it." In Pegler's world, the years before the Crash had been good not just for the rich, but for regular folks too.

Wasn't that the time when they were sticking up tall buildings in all the big towns? And building swell new suburbs and kicking out new cars by the millions, including some which retailed for around $6,000 and, what's more, selling them? Wasn't everybody working who could or would work? . . . [W]eren't ordinary, forgotten men able to fish up the price of $25 seats [for the fights] a couple of times a year? . . .

Yes, I know, the bankers and speculators and hustlers shoved us a lot of wallpaper stocks and bonds, and everybody was knocked in the creek when the wagon threw a wheel. But you wait and see what happens to Morgenthau's Mavourneens one of these days and then tell me whether, and if so why, it's any more fun to be rooked by a political party and a lot of wabble-wits stuck away in offices in Washington than by a banker. . . .

I just don't know, neighbor. For a long time when I would hear them say Old Deal in that curl-of-the-lip way I went along, too, feeling that, yes, it certainly was terrible, but let me ask you this: How were you doing back in those terrible days, and if this New Deal is going to be so swell when are those boys going to get through that long windup and let us see what they have got on the ball?

That's Westbrook Pegler in top form: sitting in the populist bully pulpit, trumpeting the cause of the corporate elite on behalf of the commoners. Not that *he* thought of it that way. Long before most Americans, rich and poor, began to fancy themselves members of the middle class, Pegler was the real deal; he embodied its contradictions and felt its bruised vanity. Pegler truly believed in his lost republic. Caught in the disorder of the Depression, he lashed out to vindicate the dispos-

sessed man in the middle, the guy who resented the freeloaders and always feared getting played for a chump by his betters.

PEGLER was born to hate. His father, a liar, a brawler, and a drunk to whom Pegler remained devoted throughout his life, loathed the rich just as Westbrook would—even as both eventually prospered as well-paid laborers for William Randolph Hearst. Arthur Pegler was credited by some as the originator of the "Hearst style," a populist tongue of blood and cliché, expressive of the sentiments of working people but emptied of any real political content. A British immigrant, the elder Pegler came of age as a member of the Boomers, a hard-drinking, wandering generation of journalists known for their inventive writing and their hatred of their own

bosses and managers. In later years, Arthur Pegler turned against even Hearst himself, writing (still in Hearst style) that Hearst papers most resembled a "screaming whore running down the street with her throat cut."

Such spectacles appealed to readers unsatisfied with the self-righteous new "objective" style of upper-middle-class papers like the *New York Times*, which, with its claim to depersonalized reality, presented itself as omniscient and unquestionable. Hearst, on the other hand, offered spicy treats, news to consume, stories that offered visceral sensation in place of critical perspective. Both approaches operated like machines built to produce particular political results, but at least yellow journalism served up some sauce along with its propaganda.

Pegler *père* spent much of his career in Chicago, home to one of America's finest political machines, and he worked hard to keep its gears well oiled. Westbrook loved his dad, and from an early age, he dreamed of taking up the same trade. He got his chance at the 1912 Republican convention in Chicago, where his career was born in a burst of disillusionment. That was the place and time, he later remarked, that America "began to go to smash."

The nineteen-year-old Pegler saw the convention as a gallery of the grotesque. Incumbent William Howard Taft's three-hundred-plus pounds symbolized to him the gluttony of a Republican Party gone rotten, and Teddy Roosevelt, whom Pegler had long admired for the way he stood up to Wall Street, revoked his promise not to run again for no other reason Pegler could discern than vanity and a feverish hunger for power.

"We stand at Armageddon, and we battle for the Lord!" TR roared, and the crowd, exhilarated by TR's "New Nationalism," screamed back in what Pegler deemed blind ecstasy. Meanwhile, Taft's "Regular" faction greased their man's path to victory. In response TR stormed out to stage his own convention just down the street. Guess who they nominated. In the months that followed, TR was shot (he survived and resumed campaigning that very day with the bullet still lodged in his chest); he decided that big business wasn't so bad after all when faced with the loss of financing from J.P. Morgan; and Taft, paralyzed by the Republican split, stayed silent. As a result Democrat Woodrow Wilson claimed the White House on a platform Pegler thought combined the worst elements of both his opponents' business appeasement and popular grandstanding.

To top it all off, the 1912 convention afforded Pegler an introduction to the Hearst empire's ace hack—an episode Pegler never forgot. He was standing around on the convention floor, he later recalled, when

> a big man with a brow like the belly of a medicine ball ripped off a few sheets of copy and, without looking up, handed them to me saying, "Boy, copy." I was a boy, but no longer a copy-boy. I was a leg man, and I tossed it back at him, saying, "Run it down yourself, I am a reporter." The Hearst super nearly died, and said, "Run that copy downstairs, or I will kill you. That is Brisbane."

As in Arthur Brisbane, the jingoistic crook whose one-sentence paragraphs

Hearst himself quoted when he wanted to say something he thought was profound. If Arthur Pegler invented the Hearst style, Brisbane was its master exploiter, using his front-page column to promote real estate schemes—just the kind of greed that Pegler could neither stomach nor ever stay altogether clear of.

If that was the moment that the United States went to smash, you might say Pegler tumbled right after. He was disposed to cheer for TR despite his misgivings, until his father explained to him that politics—and journalism—wasn't about who *should* win, but who *would* win. And when Pegler moved from politics to police court later that year, he remembered the lesson. Surveying the petty thieves, prostitutes, and down-and-outers who made up the court's clientele, Pegler saw people without power who, to his way of

thinking, didn't help themselves any by breaking the law. When it came to role models, Pegler looked to "the ham-handed sergeant of the Harrison Street station," a cop who set things right with his fists. As Pegler's biographer Oliver Pilat wrote, 1912 was when Pegler recognized that "there were two layers of people in the world, the weak and the strong; he sympathized with the weak, but he lined up with the strong."

Pegler spent the next several years bouncing from one newspaper job to another, in Des Moines, St. Louis, Dallas, Denver, and New York. He traveled to Europe to cover the First World War. But with his awkward social graces, he managed to offend every officer and editor necessary to get him booted out of the press corps. War wasn't really a good topic for him anyway; his nationalism blunted

his cynicism, without which he wrote like a blind man. Back in the States, though, he found a natural—and lucrative—journalistic niche at the ball park and beside the boxing ring.

Pegler had never been an athlete himself, aside from a few clumsy attempts at boxing, so perhaps it was his distance from the experience that allowed him to approach it with his eye on the cash register instead of the ball. He wrote that he wanted to deglamorize sports, "in rebuke to grubby box-office mercenaries." And he began turning out original stories, written for fans who felt they were getting ripped off. Readers looked to his byline as much for his skepticism as for the scores. His editors took notice, and put him on a steady schedule of raises. Pegler was getting rich.

As he joined the class he'd spent his youth loathing, Pegler continued to sharpen his knives. By 1929, Pegler was making $25,000 a year. In 1932 Hearst himself came courting, but Pegler was sitting so pretty he could afford to turn down an invitation to San Simeon to discuss contracts with the Old Man. Instead, he made a bigger move, from the sports section to the front page of the flagship Scripps-Howard paper, the *New York World-Telegram*. For $75,000, Pegler was to share Page One with Heywood Broun, each allowed to comment however he pleased on the passing scene. Broun's "It Seems to Me" was a space for liberal (and soon to be socialist) manifestos. Pegler's "Fair Enough," though, was a mystery. Pegler didn't seem to have any politics; all he had was rage.

In his second column, Pegler declared that "my hates always occupied my mind much more actively than my friendships

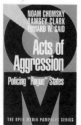

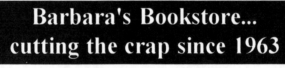

... [and] the wish to favor a friend is not so active as the instinct to annoy some person or institution I detest." Mob bosses were a sort he particularly hated, especially when such men also happened to head up unions. Although Pegler eventually came to see all unions as octopi strangling his common men with dues that went directly into their leader's bank accounts, he did pause a few times in his decades-long union-bashing rant to expose real corruption in his column. At least two well-deserved jail terms can be attributed to "Fair Enough."

Pegler carried on his campaigns in the name of one particular "little guy" known as George Spelvin, American. "Spelvin" was the stage name an actor used at the time when, in addition to his main role, he doubled in a small part. The Spelvins of the world were servants, butlers, messengers, clerks, men-on-the-street, and passersby. Pegler's Spelvin, though, was an early Archie Bunker. Union men, uppity women, swells, bubbleheads, and eventually foreigners, blacks, and Jews all gave Spelvin a stomachache.

In 1942, Spelvin went looking for a job because "Mrs. R." (Roosevelt) had "said she thought everyone should be ordered what to do by the government" and her orders were to fit into the war effort anywhere you can. Turns out, though, there were no more jobs in America that didn't require a union card, and "Bigod nobody is going to make him join anything whether it is the Elks or the Moose or the Mice or the Muskrats or whatever. It is the principle of the thing with George, and, moreover, being a native American and a veteran of the last war, he has a rather narrow prejudice against being ordered around by guys who talk like they just got off the boat."

Pegler's problem was that it was *always* the principle of the thing. He adored making stands where it was one man against the mob or the masses, and bigod, he'd go down swinging. And so he did, again and again, picking losing fights at every turn. His audience loved him for it. But Pegler failed to grasp that his readers appreciated his rants because they offered a momentary respite from the trials of their daily lives. They may have liked to hear him rail against Roosevelt's riches, but they never abandoned FDR. Pegler voiced their doubts and, in his inability to grasp the complexities of the world that shifted around him, also dissipated them. "By his own standards, he was incorruptible, honorable, and sincere," commented his biographer Pilat. "But sincerity is only an effort to gauge reality and conform to it, and his tools for that effort were inadequate." Pegler could evoke phantasms and fantasies similar to the ones that captivate countless talk radio buffs today, but when the stories were over, his readers went back to Roosevelt, unions, taxes, and the modern world—what looked to most like the only deal around.

P EGLER's hatred was pure, but it wasn't enough to save him. In the end, the contradictions of what he believed was a classless society buried him even as they made him a wealthy man. Class was Pegler's bogeyman: Even as it determined his world he refused to believe in it or to name it, calling it instead "the bosses," then "the unions," and finally "the Communists" he seemed to see everywhere in his old age.

By then he'd gone over to Hearst and beyond. In 1943, the National Maritime Union had put a thousand pickets around the *World-Telegram* to protest a column he'd written about what he considered the royal wages of union seamen. The paper's publisher, Roy Howard, decided Pegler had to go. Pegler agreed; he'd recently received another offer from Hearst, and despite his longstanding personal affection for Howard, he relished the jump in pay and readers. *Newsweek* estimated that the new job would give him access to ten million loyalists; Hearst salesmen quadrupled the figure.

But Pegler remained, in Murray Kempton's words, "the man who hated publishers," and in the end he couldn't spare Hearst his scorn. After two decades of selling Citizen Kane's papers with a column that increasingly resembled a blast furnace; after turning against the Newspaper Guild, the one union to which he'd held a little bit of loyalty; after abandoning the religious tolerance of his youth in favor of ever more obvious and loathsome anti-Semitism (international bankers and "prophets" came to be staple fare); after staking Joe McCarthy to a run with relentless good press and watching him tire on the rail, Pegler came around at last to the original enemy, the boss.

When Pegler was a younger man, the boss of bosses had been Hearst Senior himself—in Pegler's words at the time, "the leading American fascist." By 1962, almost two decades into the Cold War, Pegler allowed himself to praise Old Man Hearst as a "great founding genius." The problem now was his son, W.R. Hearst Jr. Before the thirty-five hundred members of the Anti-Communist Christian Crusade in Tulsa, in a speech warning of a new "coercion" that ruled the press, Pegler excoriated the younger Hearst for lacking "character, ability, loyalty, and principle."

No doubt Hearst did. But he shared his father's intolerance of dissent, and the next day Pegler was banished from mainstream journalism forever. By then, he may not have cared, for he had observed throughout the Fifties the degeneration of the newspaper columnist's craft into assembly-line production of "packaged goods" designed by the publisher. Pegler had discovered that newspapers were becoming indistinguishable from other branches of the entertainment industry. His own employer, King Features, was, as he described it to the audience in Tulsa, "a subdivision of the Hearst empire dealing in comic books, comic strip books, sweet powders to make soda pop, toys, and a very ingenious variety of dingbats for the immature."

Pegler liked to say again and again that he was no egghead (he barely finished high school), but at times there's a strange subtlety to his beliefs that almost resembles the ideas of the German-Jewish leftist philosopher Theodor Adorno. A refugee from the Third Reich, Adorno understood better than most that a million fans *can* be wrong. In "The Culture Industry: Enlightenment as Mass Deception," an essay co-written with Max Horkheimer and published in 1944, Adorno observed that "culture now impresses the same stamp on everything.... Even the aesthetic activities of political opposites are one in their enthusiastic obedience to the rhythm of the iron system.... Under monopoly all mass culture is identical, and the lines of the artificial framework begin to show through."

Pegler could have written that passage, though he would have done so in the purple prose of alliteration and anger. Unlike the demagogues of today's backlash, who rail against cultural elites even as they lend aid and comfort to Republican revolutionists, Pegler was his own man. He understood that the politics of corruption and power lust, practiced by Democrats and Republicans alike, dulled people to independent thinking, made them susceptible to slogans and contented with "color-press pictures of pretty models in glove-tight swimming suits in the ads." For Pegler's part, that was reason enough to hate the bosses, whoever they were.

BY THE time he was blacklisted, Pegler had already exiled himself, setting up a private retreat in the desert outside Tucson. From there he cultivated a revolving roster of rich men with far-right views who adopted Pegler for various dubious journalistic endeavors. But not even crackpot rags like the John Birch Society's *American Opinion* could contain Pegler's obsession: Its editor finally ended the relationship, complaining of the "monotony of Pegler's articles" about the twin demons, Eleanor and Earl (Roosevelt and Warren). His next employer, a conservative business monthly called the *Toledo Monitor*, begged him to lay off "1) New Deal & Roosevelts; 2) Kennedys; 3) Jews." Not long after he lost one of his last jobs, his beloved wife died. Although Pegler married twice again, from there on out he was alone, and his loneliness made him even meaner. He fought his distant desert neighbors over the howling of their dogs. He brawled in the streets of Tucson. Much of what he wrote was no longer publishable, but he sat in his empty, pure, American landscape pounding out more and more of it, trying to get at the monster he couldn't name.

In 1966, when the *New York Herald Tribune*, *World-Telegram*, and *Journal-American* all died, Pegler wrote to Kempton, one of his last friends: "If you have a spare half-hour, please write what happened to our world. Peg."

Three years later Pegler died too, without ever realizing what had happened to the once-dazzling cosmos of journalism in which his uncompromising columns had shone. The masters he willingly served (even as he thought he fought them) had killed it. He had helped.

Pegler went to his death a true believer in his own virtue, broken and uncomprehending. His life epitomized the conservative backlash of the Cold War—a tragedy made in no small part by real adversity and fear. That grim episode has passed, but the spirit of Pegler has returned as a faux-populist puppet show, with the "common people" reduced to one of Rush's props. When Pegler was busy raging against fat cats and fascists, and holding forth on the unbearable arrogance of power, he hit some nice notes. Those columns still offer an insight for both readers and reporters: the civic virtues of well-tuned fury.

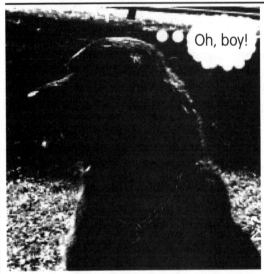

CREAM CITY CONFIDENTIAL

The Black-baiting of Milwaukee's Last Pink Mayor

Jim Arndorfer

A TRIP down North Avenue tells more about Milwaukee than any tour guide could. The four-lane commercial artery begins near an enclave of palatial houses overlooking Lake Michigan and some five miles to the west empties into the leafy suburb of Wauwatosa, followed by the even shadier lanes of Brookfield and Elm Grove. The people in both places are overwhelmingly white. Most of what lies in between is the so-called Core, a stretch of blight and decay that could be traced from a generic template for ghettoes in nearly every large American city: urban meadows, liquor stores, boarded-up buildings, and discount shops. Most of the faces here—need it be said?—are black.

I grew up near North Avenue on the West Side of Milwaukee in a predominantly white middle-class neighborhood of duplexes and bungalows that stood as a buffer zone between the Core and those with cash. Neighbors looked west with a mix of aspiration and envy and saw a Shangri-la; they looked east and saw a cesspool that needed to be contained lest it engulf them. Back then this attitude—this was during the Seventies and Eighties, mind you—was vividly expressed in everyday conversation. One adult I knew wanted to wall off the black neighborhood; another said he wouldn't mind if someone dropped a neutron bomb there.

The ugly history of Milwaukee race relations was speaking through these people. When accounting for the city's racial and economic polarization, there is certainly enough blame to go around: It is the legacy of average white Milwaukeeans refusing to live and sometimes to work side by side with African Americans; of city officials refusing to accommodate them; of employers reluctant to hire them and banks to lend to them; and of real estate companies to sell or rent them decent housing. Milwaukee's is such a familiar story that it's tempting to regard the degradation of American cities (now that we're all supposed to be post-racists) as a tragic episode of mass irrationality—lumpen prejudice run amok—combined with inexorable economic and demographic forces playing themselves out.

But it's worth remembering, too, that popular racism was a bludgeon used to great effect by economic and political elites, not only for immediate ends such as breaking a strike or winning an election but to exclude certain issues from public

Jim Arndorfer is a business reporter. He lives in Chicago.

69

debate altogether. Indeed, as the great postwar migration of Southern blacks intensified racial friction in Northern cities, the few brave political leaders of the center and the left who called for tolerance did so at their peril. Frank Zeidler, the popular mayor of Milwaukee throughout the prosperous Fifties, was one such leader. Zeidler urged Milwaukeeans to face the challenge of absorbing the latest wave of immigrants, proposing among other things an ambitious plan for the construction of new public housing. It was his political undoing. By the time Zeidler bowed out of city politics in 1960, he had been wearied by a race-baiting campaign so ferocious it made national headlines.

Race, however, was only the proximate cause of Zeidler's undoing. He had another black mark against him, at least in the book of Milwaukee's business leaders and their pawns on the Common Council: He was a Socialist, and he'd done plenty to get on their bad side. Before they race-baited him, Zeidler's enemies redbaited him. But Milwaukee was the kind of place where *that* message fell on deaf ears: Its citizens had been giving their votes to reds for decades. Backed by German skilled workers, other immigrant groups, and labor, the Milwaukee Socialists (officially the Social Democratic Party) first came to prominence in the elections of 1910 when they captured virtually every important office of the city and sent the first Socialist to the U.S. House of Representatives. Their victory mirrored the cresting of the Socialist movement across the country. Between 1910 and 1911, seventy-four cities and towns elected Socialists as mayors or other major municipal officers; eleven states elected Socialists to their legislatures. The Milwaukee Socialists were pragmatic, clean-government reformers who supported unions, expanded city and social services, and instituted health programs; their focus on these commonplace concerns earned them the pejorative nickname "Sewer Socialists" from more radical leftists. After the First World War Socialist politicians began to disappear across the nation as the government cracked down and party factions squabbled. But not in Milwaukee. There Socialist Daniel W. Hoan, appealing to a broad cross-section of the population, held office as mayor from 1916 until 1940, when he was defeated by a Republican—one Carl Zeidler, the older brother of Frank.

The once-proud Social Democratic Party crumbled within a few years after Hoan's defeat, its dejected members fleeing to the ranks of the Democratic and Progressive parties. Then along came Frank Zeidler. The slight and soft-spoken Zeidler joined the Socialists in 1932 at the age of twenty; the ravages of the Depression convinced him society needed to change, and the cooperative vision of Socialist writers Norman Thomas and Kirby Page captivated him. Within a few years he was elected county surveyor and he went on to serve on the city school board. He ran for mayor in 1944 as a Socialist but lacked sufficient support to get past the nonpartisan mayoral primary. Undeterred, he ran again four years later, this time as an independent backed by group of labor leaders, old Socialists, liberal Democrats, and even a group of Republicans called the Municipal Enterprise

Committee. The city's newspapers and business interests, fearful that socialism was returning to Milwaukee, lashed out at Zeidler, more because of his political affiliation than any unpalatable Bolshevik ideas. A *Milwaukee Journal* columnist thundered: "Frank Zeidler is no Communist, but in these dangerous times HIS SOCIALIST COLLECTIVISM WOULD WEAKEN OUR DEFENSES AGAINST THE COLLECTIVISM OF STALIN." Rival Henry Reuss brazenly charged that Zeidler "thinks the city ought to be running the corner grocery store." No amount of red-baiting made a difference. Backed by labor—and helped, ironically, by the name connection to his brother, who was killed in action during the Second World War—Zeidler won.

As mayor, Zeidler literally reshaped Milwaukee. Looking for room for new industry and housing, he embarked on an aggressive annexation program that ultimately doubled the size of the city and boosted its population to 750,000. He raised a sports arena as well as County Stadium for the Milwaukee Braves. He built up the library system, helped establish a public television station, erected affordable housing, enhanced the park system, and expanded and improved public services. He did it all, despite a reliably hostile Common Council, by striking alliances with liberal Democrats and Republicans and often governing by threat of veto. There weren't any Socialist aldermen, and the council shot down any Socialists or ex-Socialists Zeidler nominated for city offices. He rallied popular support with a grueling public speaking schedule, making up to three hundred appearances a year.

While Zeidler was popular with the people—he was re-elected in 1952 with 72 percent of the vote—the city's business community hated him. His desire to impose public ownership on the city's utility and mass transit companies terrified them. His drive to build low-income housing infuriated the real estate industry. He was disturbingly pro-union; in 1955 he refused to let a freighter in the Milwaukee harbor unload clay and materials destined for the Kohler Co. in Sheboygan, then embroiled in a bitter strike. Besides, he was a damned Socialist who had the gall to point out that protective laws and subsidies made a mockery of the words "free competition." Nevertheless, between his policies of suburban annexation and building projects such as County

RADICAL MADISON

PAUL BUHLE

Madison, Wisconsin was by no means the Athens of the Midwest—unless Athens is badly overrated—but it looked awfully good to a homegrown Marxist from downstate Illinois in August 1967. In Champaign of unhappy memory, a mucky green-bottomed swamp passed for a picturesque body of water, and lovers (presumably either married or chaste) rowed around when the summer heat became too unbearable for any other activity. Madison, meanwhile, had five lakes, the big ones then suffering only mildly from agricultural runoff, and lovers of unrestricted if not perhaps unlimited variety on the campus side. Besides, Madison had so many peaceniks, left-wing intellectuals, bohemians, and just plain Jewish liberals that I felt more at home, the first week there, than in twenty years of my old neighborhoods.

One of the best and most recognizable aspects of Madison was its left/right confusion and its deeply upper Midwestern prejudices. There were Swiss communities in close driving distance which had voted in referenda against U.S. participation in both world wars, the

Korean War, and Vietnam. The city's newspaper, the *Capital Times*, had in fact been launched to oppose the earliest "war to end all wars," even if it had lost most of its sense of tradition fifty years later. The local right was made up of the usual real estate interests, bankers, and bright-faced suburbanites. But even here, among Joe McCarthy's old admirers, the suspicion of the State and its imperial machinations was not quite the same as it had been in conservative Champaign—or for that matter in ostensibly liberal New York. Isolationism had never really died in the North Country.[†]

Besides, here I had numbers on my side. In Champaign, leading a peace demonstration would get you Minuteman stickers ("You are in the sights of a Minuteman") on your mailbox and the occasional threatening phone call; in Madison, there were too many reds and too many types of reds for the rednecks to nail.

Here the right had to learn to live with institutions like the leftish student eating co-ops, disproportionately Jewish, which had carried on from one generation to another since the Thirties. Here, antifascism had been the soul of the Good War effort. But came a Bad War, and all sorts gathered on a common

---

† Actually, the story is a bit more complicated. Northern Wisconsin, along with Long Island, was the epicenter of the pro-Nazi American Bund during the Thirties. McCarthy, like Richard Nixon, made a spirited effort after the war to paint former Bundists as patriots, as well as to protect ex-Nazis or collaborators who managed to emigrate to America. But even at the height of his popularity, McCarthy was careful not to go after the University of Wisconsin: It was too close to home, its success too vital for the state's collective pride and economic advancement. Miniature McCarthys in the state legislature had long made a name for themselves attacking "red professors" corrupting Wisconsin children, but their influence was never great.

Stadium, Zeidler was often enough regarded as a boon to city business. Indeed, in 1958 *Fortune* magazine declared Milwaukee to be the second-best-run city in the country.

In 1956 Zeidler's opposition—which was bipartisan in the truest sense of the word—fielded their strongest candidate to date against the mayor: conservative Democrat Milton J. McGuire, the president of the Common Council and a partisan of the city's corporate interests. When he announced his candidacy in January, McGuire made the usual Bolshevik-bashing noises. He condemned Zeidler for his "socialistic utterances" and for being "pro-labor union"; moreover, he claimed Zeidler's politics prevented the city from getting its fair share of federal or state pork. In defense of the free enterprise system, he noted that there were more radios and TV sets in Milwaukee than "any of those socialist countries like Norway."

McGuire and his supporters must have soon discovered

that this tired rhetoric wasn't hitting home, so they played a different card: race. Milwaukee was a city of homeowners, and it was easy to convince even well-meaning liberals that the influx of African-Americans would lower their property values. In fact, the mayor's enemies had already been laying the entire blame for the Great Migration on Zeidler for years. A small African-American community had existed in Milwaukee since the nineteenth century, but it didn't start growing significantly until the Forties. From 1950 to 1960 the black population tripled to about sixty thousand. When the ghetto of the Inner Core slowly but surely started expanding, real estate agents swooped down on bordering neighborhoods to blockbust. One of their favorite lines: Zeidler was going to import blacks into the neighborhood. In 1952 an old woman grabbed Zeidler at a meeting and demanded to know, "Why are you making me sell my home? My real estate agent told me you were going to make us sell our homes to Negroes." Still Zeidler stuck to his guns. "I made many speeches saying that no matter what color you were, everybody deserved equal rights and opportunities," Zeidler, now eighty-seven, recalls. "That's when I was threatened." Police had to stand watch outside his house.

McGuire supporters revived weel-worn rumors and made up some new ones. One piece of gossip claimed Zeidler's oldest daughter was married to a black man; another claimed Zeidler was posting billboards in the South urging African Americans to move up to Milwaukee. This rumor, which first surfaced in taverns across the city back in 1952, was believed by tens of thousands of people. With Zeidler campaign supporters getting jeered as "nigger lovers," the Milwaukee Federated Trades Council asked unions in ten Southern states to look for these mythical billboards. Not surprisingly, no signs were found; nor were the rumormongers.

The McGuire campaign was so repulsive that even *Time* magazine felt the need to defend a Socialist. It ran a brief story praising Zeidler for behaving "more like a conservative burgomaster than a doctrinaire Socialist" and shot down the rumors. Though McGuire may have denounced the charges as "shameful," the piece pointed out, he "undoubtedly stands to benefit from the whispering campaign against Zeidler." In fact, McGuire fanned white Milwaukee's racial

ground. Now the children of liberal Republicans (like myself), the children of erstwhile reds, and Milwaukeeans whose parents had elected a Socialist mayor as recently as the Fifties learned that they had a lot in common.

At any rate, this was the right place for my new journal, *Radical America*, which I'd launched (one mediocre issue) back East while taking a master's in history. Here I had instant comrades, more Wobbly than Communist in sentiment, including a Movement printer with a single-sheet press (purchased, I learned later, with revenues from staging the theatrical satire *MacBird*). I even had a mailing list, supplied by the Radical Education Project of Students for a Democratic Society (SDS). Within a year or so, the magazine had reached a readership between two and three thousand, drawing the interest of a mixture of students, old radicals, and assorted intelligence analysts. Occasional "special issues" on women's history, culture, or black labor ran considerably higher.

The basic idea of the magazine was in the name (perhaps), a play upon the title of a novel by Harvey Swados, *A Radical's America*. I had made up my mind that there was a radical heritage to be found here at home, and that no pondering of exotic (i.e., European) theory could substitute for that native tradition. Believing this demanded a certain credulity: In the U.S., homegrown rebels are more likely to be utopians, peaceniks, abolitionists, free lovers, gay lovers, or rawboned spiritualists than labor militants— more petty bourgeois or underemployed than proletarian.

But it struck a chord. Pretty soon, from a second-story apartment in a picturesque working-class neighborhood not far from the water, I was A Man of Letters, at least in that I wrote them by the hundreds and got responses from the likes of Jack

London's daughter Joan, Daniel De Leon's son Solon (expelled from his father's Socialist Labor Party in 1913, it was said, for questioning the labor theory of value), Anna Louise Strong (the Seattle Sunday school teacher who had resettled first in Russia then China), and others young and old to whom radical history meant something special.

For a while I did virtually everything but the printing myself: dragging boxes of paper to the press (in a VW), taking pages to an SDS group house for collating (I supplied the good Wisconsin beer), stuffing the mailing bags for bulk orders and envelopes for subs, sending out bills, and keeping a steady correspondence going with "Associates." These latter were types similar to myself, grad students or dropouts who worked in the off-campus bookshops, took part in mobilizations of all kinds, and had similar intellectual interests, from Johnny Appleseed to Antonio Gramsci. I had the time. The student strikes got me out of teaching for long spells, while my own classes and assorted political work didn't get in the way too much. Besides, I was suited to working at home even when the romantic political role models of the day were traveling from city to city and coed to coed.

I like to think of my circle of friends, expanded into an editorial board by 1970, as a collection of young left-wing oddballs. My most reliable comrade was Jim, son of the president of a Southern black college and inveterate organizer of left-wing study classes on campus. Poetry editor Dave was a Nietzchean who went to work as a reporter at the *Capital Times* and eventually led the 1979-80 strike that got him blacklisted from the trade. One of our women's history specialists was Edie, a survivor of the Japanese-American internment camps; another was Ann, a grad

paranoia in a slightly more polite fashion, particularly during the debate over public housing. Milwaukee was straining under a postwar housing shortage, and Zeidler hoped to relieve it by building ten thousand units of public housing, some of it low-income. Reactionaries had previously opposed public housing on the grounds it was socialistic; now they opposed it because it would encourage African Americans to move into the city. Indeed, Edward Plantz, head of the Milwaukee County Property Owners' Association, didn't even bother to mask his reasons for opposing Zeidler's slum clearance and public housing plans: "I call a spade a spade. If there is more housing, more people will move into Milwaukee. The only thing that has kept . . . Negroes from coming up there is the lack of housing." McGuire didn't use the word "spade," but everyone knew his targets when—amazingly enough, in a speech before the NAACP— he said that: "Some have stated that newcomers come here because Milwaukee is a soft touch. A person can be here a day and get relief. I favor a law requiring longer residence." Time limits should also be imposed on how long families

stayed in housing—with veterans and widows excepted of course. Otherwise, McGuire reasoned, people would turn down raises so they could stay in public housing.

McGuire—whose campaign repertoire actually included the slogan "Milwaukee needs an honest white man for mayor"—ultimately may have been undone by his own bigotry. Despite Milwaukee's low crime rate, the McGuire for Mayor Committee sought to play on fears of rampaging African-American youth with an ad that claimed "hoodlum mobs [are] ranging Milwaukee with wolf pack viciousness." The ad, understandably, angered cops—who by and large were McGuire supporters—and drew rebukes from the city's police chief and district attorney. South Side Republican alderman Anthony J. Gruszka, no friend of Zeidler or socialism, accused McGuire of running a "Nazi" campaign, citing its "injection of racism, the condemnation of our youth, and the criticism of our police agencies."

Surprising many, including himself, Zeidler won the 1956 election, although by a very narrow margin. The victory was short-lived, however. The bitterness of the campaign and continued battles over public housing—including a failed bid to build low-income housing in the city's predominantly blue-collar South Side—persuaded Zeidler not to run for a fourth term in 1960. "My health could not stand another vicious campaign such as that I had to engage in with Alderman McGuire in 1956 on the housing issue and the race question," he wrote in his unpublished memoirs, which are now kept in the Milwaukee Public Library. "And this issue certainly would have been raised again in the 1960 campaign." He once hoped to build ten thousand units of public housing; he managed to build thirty-two hundred.

The 1956 election taught Milwaukee politicians the dangers of being friendly to African Americans. The twenty-eight-year reign of Zeidler's successor, Henry Maier, proved to be a lesson in denial. Immediately after taking office, he shelved a report on the Core commissioned by Zeidler that, among other things, urged outreach programs for youth and job-training for adults. Subsequently, Maier put a two-year freeze on public housing construction to "review" the situation. In 1963 he warned his community relations commission to go slow on civil rights. He opposed the open-housing ordinances that Vel Phillips, Milwaukee's first black al-

student and sometime editor of the local underground press, who later married a Teamster leader known as the "Lenin of Dane County"; another was Mari Jo, a Polish-American blue-collar girl from a Little Steel town in northern Illinois (later a MacArthur Fellow); and still another, a collaborator on our second biggest special issue (on women's history), was Nancy, now the president of Oberlin College. Smart people, none of them in the Old Left mold.

I said the second biggest hit, because the biggest was *Radical America Komiks,* a product of my childhood love for *Mad Comics* (which preceded *Mad Magazine* and was funnier) and the chance appearance in Madison of *Feds 'n' Heads,* brainchild of dropout grad student Gilbert Shelton. I sold Shelton's antic comic (arguably the very first "Underground" comic and the one which introduced the Fabulous Furry Freak Brothers) at the SDS table in the student union, and when one day I received a couple thousand dollars from the Rabinowitz Foundation (whose dwindling financial legacy stemmed from, if I remember correctly, the patent on a bra snap), I turned it over immediately to Gilbert. He set up Rip Off Press in San Franciso, and his first production was *Radical America Komiks.* It lacked Crumb (a big disappointment to me) but was full of a kind of dopey verve. The center spread was gory class war: "The Meth Freaks Fight the Feds to the Finish."

Meanwhile, we had "discovered" my favorite adopted mentor, the aged political athlete C.L.R. James. This former cricket star and champion broad jumper from Trinidad had been part of the first wave of West Indian literary intellectuals in the Twenties, had written *The Black Jacobins* (the story of the Haitian revolution of the 1790s), become a noted Marxist philosopher, got himself expelled from the United States during the McCarthy period, wrote a great political book on sports (*Beyond a Boundary*) and was now the last old-time Pan Africanist on the lecture circuit. He was also a smooth culture critic and a keen observer of daily working-class life—just what we needed for our revolutionary optimism about insurgent culture and (we hoped) the return of social struggle à la the Thirties, without a domineering Communist Party, naturally.

I remember James best in the restaurant of a once grand, now seedy Madison hotel, drinking tea with milk and spreading marmalade on his toast, British style, before setting off to wow a circle of admirers with running commentaries on classical art, Hegel, Black Power, and the insurrectionary impulses of Parisian workers and students during May 1968. He only came to Madison now and then, but his aura surrounded us, perhaps because, like Madison itself, he was so far off the usual map.

Of course things never worked out the way we thought they would in some great global burst of freedom. And yet there were isolated victories. My teaching stint ended, ironically, just as the Teaching Assistants Association nearly won a major strike against the university and began working to send its vigorous new leaders to the head of the local labor federation and eventually the state AFL-CIO. Madison was in many ways a good place to be during the torpid Seventies, frozen in time with a radical mayor and a drastically reformed police force. But I was only a summer visitor in those latter days, past going back.

Even so, I have never stopped feeling that leaving the Midwest a second time was the biggest mistake that I have ever made. What I should have been doing—what we all should have been doing in 1971—was looking for a

derman, introduced into the Council four times between 1962 and 1967; each of the proposals—which merely mirrored state law—was shot down eighteen to one. City-only housing ordinances would encourage white flight, Maier reasoned; the suburbs would have to open first. This neglect caused resentment in the black neighborhoods, and protests over housing and school segregation flared during the early Sixties. A riot broke out in the summer of 1967, leaving three dead. Maier pinned the blame on "so-called civil rights leaders who have been encouraging defiance of the law." That same year, Roman Catholic priest James Groppi and the NAACP Youth Council started two hundred days of open-housing marches, frequently targeting the highly segregated South Side. They were met by thousands of bottle-hurling whites. Known during the nineteenth century as the "German Athens" for its vibrant cultural life, or as the "Cream City" for the color of the brick used in its buildings, Milwaukee found itself tagged with another nickname: "The Selma of the North."

Would racial harmony have flourished in Milwaukee had Zeidler remained in office? Perhaps not. Zeidler's critics have pointed out that, for all his good intentions and his rhetoric, he did little to address job discrimination, school segregation, or housing discrimination. Even if he had tried, it's likely the Common Council would have stymied him again and again. Yet rhetoric and intentions do have consequences. Zeidler at the very least sought to establish a dialogue about how African Americans could be brought into the mainstream of Milwaukee society. Once he stepped down, succeeding politicians deemed it expedient—as had McGuire—to score points with some members of the white community by ignoring or taking a stand against the city's burgeoning African-American population. This tactic proved to be one of gradual suicide as the black population of Milwaukee steadily grew. The white population, meanwhile, cast its ballot for the city's future by pressing their feet against gas pedals en route to the suburbs.

Milwaukee had a population of 750,000 when Zeidler left office; it has since shrunk to about 600,000. Roughly a third of its people are now African American, as the white flight that started during the Fifties continues. When integration came to my neighborhood in the Seventies, hatred of African Americans was part of the air I breathed. "There's too many niggers around here," said a childhood friend, visiting the block after his parents fled. A grade school classmate was thrown out of class for chanting "nigger" during a filmstrip about Martin Luther King Jr. "He had the right to say what he wanted to, so why can't I?" my classmate demanded to know, anticipating the backlash against so-called political correctness by a decade. He is now a Milwaukee cop.

In the first half of this century, the Milwaukee Socialists, "Fighting Bob" La Follette, and a militant labor movement made Wisconsin a showplace of progressive politics. The state introduced the country's first laws for workmen's compensation and the minimum wage, among many other reforms.

That's changed. From the Fifties of Joe McCarthy and Milton McGuire to Governor Tommy Thompson's Nineties, Wisconsin has led the union in the politics of backlash. "Power to the People" is still the cry (it was even the title of Thompson's 1996 book), but between the state's war on welfare and campaign against public education, power to the wealthy and more comfort to the comfortable is the result.

place to make a stand, to go on contesting power and looking for new possibilities. I'm pretty sure, looking back, that I would have been more effective as a homeboy, within at least my regional world if not my literal hometown.

Maintaining that vision of homegrown radicalism has grown more relevant than ever in the years since then. There is no such thing as Far Away in the global market, and Americans remain the country club set of the planet, as blind or indifferent to the cost of their golf course existence as the frat boys and debs back in dear old Champaign. We need to awaken to ourselves, to our disappearing jobs (returned as low-wage and second-tier work), to our vast prison industry, to the limits of environmental expropriation, and to the reality of a drastically changed working class, increasingly female and nonwhite. Our national saga and the story of radicalism is expanding far beyond *Radical America*'s perspective, including Emilio Zapata along with Eugene Debs and Martin Luther King Jr.

The history of American radicalism has always been profoundly discontinuous: Only a few times in a century can we expect millions of ordinary folks to exclaim, "I've been lied to all my life!" Little magazines will doubtless continue to have an outsized role in the wake-up process. While their big, slick cousins organize themselves in terms of advertising dollars or the prestige needed for more of the same, the little magazines go about attracting the acid iconoclasts, the homespun utopians and the creative cranks needed to break through the layers of ideological detritus accumulated since the last wave of challenges. *Radical America*'s sun has set, but there are always new figures moving along the horizon.

HOLLYWOOD'S CORPORATE ART

JEROME CHRISTENSEN

MEN don't make movies. Industries don't make movies. Corporations do. Hollywood studios make films not only to achieve the usual corporate goals of profit and prestige, but also to advertise, to tell audiences what kind of institution the corporation would like to be and to describe the kind of social role that the corporation would like to have. Hollywood's speech is corporate speech, with a distinctly populist inflection. Its studios make products that represent corporate interests as the inchoate aspirations of the people. They contrive to form a people happy to be incorporated as an audience and gratified to want what the studios devise, tout, and screen. This corporate populist formula was established in the early sound era, as the studios of the Thirties confected and propagated an American popular culture which was and is the culture of the corporation.

No commentator of the first two decades of the century could mistake the growing economic power of the modern corporation. But after the Crash in 1929, numerous observers began to worry about the absence of any guiding economic intelligence that could keep the engine of capital from combusting the social fuel that sustained it. Surveying the industrial scene in 1932, Reinhold Niebuhr lamented the "lack of social intelligence in all of our economic groups," and gloomily concluded that "power is never checked by the voluntary action of those who hold it but only by raising power against it." Niebuhr turned out to be wrong. Corporate America did check its power, if only briefly, when company after company signed on to cooperate in the National Recovery Administration, the New Deal's solution to disastrous competition. But voluntary cooperation with federal regulators was not enough to redeem big business in the eyes of the public. The Thirties were marked by an unprecedented hostility to big business, as politicians, labor leaders, and journalists denounced the "soulless" corporation. Corporations responded, as historian Roland Marchand has shown, with "institutional" advertising campaigns that imagined the likes of GM and U.S. Steel as neighbors and friends, people just like everyone else.

How did businessmen know what people were like? They went to the movies just like everyone else. What they saw

Jerome Christensen is Professor of English at Vanderbilt University.

there, what everyone saw there, was a novel and practically irresistible form of institutional advertising—brilliantly contrived, glamorously mounted tableaux of the social world as the Hollywood studios saw it. Whatever else they did, Hollywood films worked obliquely but relentlessly to promote the Hollywood studio as the business uniquely endowed with social intelligence. They formulated and expressed the needs and desires of an audience that encompassed businessmen and immigrant laborers alike. More importantly, they advertised a new culture of the studios' creation, a place in which corporations could make themselves at home, in which the corporation would be indistinguishable from the people. The Supreme Court had bestowed upon the corporation the legal status of a person; the Hollywood movie made it a natural fact.

Niebuhr overlooked the role of Hollywood in generating the cultural intelligence so critical to the survival and prosperity of corporate capitalism, but *Fortune* magazine did not. In 1932 it profiled MGM as the studio whose moving pictures made manifest the destiny of the American corporation:

> MGM is neither one man nor a collection of men. It is a corporation. Whenever a motion picture becomes a work of art it is unquestionably due to men. But the moving picture has been born and bred not of men but of corporations. Corporations have set up the easels, bought the pigments, arranged the views, and hired the potential artists. Until the artists emerge, at least, the corporation is bigger than the sum of its parts. Somehow, although our poets have not yet defined it for us, a corporation

lives a life and finds a fate outside the lives and fates of its human constituents.

Fortune's respectful consideration of MGM's corporate status was unusual. By ordinary standards of accounting the motion picture corporations were extraordinarily profitable, but they hardly rivaled the likes of General Motors and DuPont as bulwarks of the economy. But in the face of widespread overproduction—of all-too tangible factories idle and empty, of tangible inventories clogging tangible warehouses—the sheer mass of industrial capital suddenly counted less than the intangible "it" that gave Hollywood access to the hearts and minds and pockets of the consumer.

> For the central fact about a movie producing company is the legal unreality of its assets. No matter how expensive, Paramount's collection of cameras, contracts, and miscellaneous property is as useless as the negative of last year's program picture without that hugely flickering intangible, its value as a going concern. Which resides not in Celluloid and brick but in the smiles of stars, the vitality of stories, the guts of producers, the shrewdness of salesmen, the digestions of exhibitors. Not only is the product itself a mere shadowed dream, but its manufacture and its routes to an unpredictable market . . . are zigzagged with maybes and haunted by states of mind.

Then as now Hollywood films were as much the calculated revelations of the aims of the studios that made them as they were the product of writers', directors', or producers' genius. They were the medium through which studios revealed their agendas and sought to realize them.

Through their movies the studios stated what they wanted from other studios and other industries, from their labor force and managers, from exhibitors and distributors, from the government and from their customers. Through movies the studios sought to mold their audiences into the kind of people who wanted what the studios wanted, what the corporations wanted. Hollywood art was and is corporate art; and corporate art, whether in the specific form of institutional advertising or in its broader cast as public relations, is allegorical: It says one thing while meaning many other things; it manifestly addresses one audience—say, the administrator of the famous male gaze—while covertly addressing numerous others: vigilant censors, truculent stars, gung ho trustbusters, corporate players, and Midwestern garden clubs.

Consider *The Nuisance*, an MGM picture that appeared in early 1933 when American corporations, already unnerved by the Depression, fearfully awaited the coming of the New Deal. At the outset the protagonist, a shyster personal injury

attorney and ambulance chaser by the name of J. Phineas Stevens, defends himself against the imputation that he is a shyster lawyer and ambulance chaser with the sarcastic claim that he is only "seeking justice from the soulless corporation on behalf of the forgotten man and the forgotten woman." Later, in court, defending a client under indictment for stealing from his employer, the Street Railway Company, Stevens again denounces the "soulless corporation." Such anti-corporate talk, complete with references to FDR's famous "forgotten man," clearly signaled a political commitment. Except that Stevens is openly cynical: He does not believe a word he says.

The narrative leaves no doubt about Stevens's cynicism, but neither does it try to prove that the Railway Company has a soul. The corporation lawyer's tactics are fully as unethical as the shyster's. He hires a pretty girl to entrap Stevens and collect incriminating evidence. Stevens does eventually get hauled into court, but he escapes conviction by marrying the corporation's plant, thus blocking her testimony. When

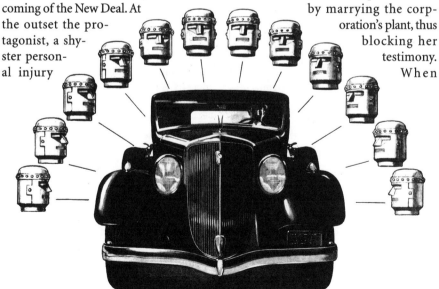

the prosecutor retaliates by jailing the turncoat bride for perjury Stevens finagles her release. Having seen his only friend die and his wife go to jail as direct consequences of his chicanery, he solemnly promises his bride "no more ambulance chasing." It's not long, however, before Stevens falls off the wagon and hands his business card to a "flopper" who has just staged an accident on the street. The film ends on a note as cynical as that with which it began.

The Nuisance makes no brief against the social order. On the contrary, the film argues that laws are necessary because corporations, even "soulless" ones, are necessary. Personal injury lawyers depend on the prosperity of corporations, whose liability the law defines. In *The Nuisance* the soulless corporation pays everyone, whether in wages, settlements, or damages. And because both the corporation and Stevens are in business only for the money, Stevens's adversarial practice implies no adversarial politics. However he might play the "soullessness" card, as long as he stays in the legal game he is the corporation's witting accomplice. And why not? Without corporations accidents would still happen. It's just that there would be nobody to pay the damages. Personal injury law may be a mild form of distributive justice, but not only is it better than none at all, for the principals it surpasses any other. Thus Stevens fits in a world where the evolved corporate mode of production is manifestly necessary. As if to demonstrate that the Railway Company hurts people only accidentally—that it has nothing to do with the profit motive—the film tolerates the incidental staging of accidents as part of the cost of doing corporate business. Whatever is profitable is right. Pain and suffering may occur, but accidentally, not necessarily. And once damages are paid off, accidents no longer count; they have no history.

But why a lawyer? All lawyers may be cynics, but a cynic need not be a lawyer. The answer seems to be that as a fee-driven attorney, Stevens's sophistries become a form of commercial speech—as is a motion picture, according to a Supreme Court ruling of 1915. In the Thirties commercial speech was a kind of quasi-legal speech; it could be published, broadcast, and screened, but it was not protected in the way individual citizens were when they published or broadcast their speech. Precisely because the Supreme Court would not protect commercial speech against the outrage of moralists or the opportunism of politicians, MGM had a considerable interest in doing so (as studios still have today). In *The Nuisance* MGM addresses its audience in commercial speech on behalf of commercial speech as socially serviceable, worthy of legal protection if not constitutional immunity. A toleration of cynicism counts as a defense of a business in which making a living requires continuous manipulation of the law.

You can learn a lot about the world of the Thirties by studying MGM, but you inevitably learn about MGM's world. RKO cared about nightclub life in New York; Fox about narratives as tight as its budget; Paramount about the decor of its sets, the temperament of its directors, and the ambitions of its writers. When Warner Bros. depicted nightclubs or the rackets or the big house or the assembly line, it was looking for metaphors to figure the business of making movies that make money. The golddigger worked, offstage and on, to get either a paycheck or a sugar daddy.

MGM, meanwhile, cared about an America fashioned in the likeness of MGM's own happy corporate family. MGM projected its organizational profile on the law, the theater, politics, and the family to show that human interest depends on its similarity to the motion picture industry, on people's organized capacity to be entertaining. In *Fortune's* epitome, Warner Bros.' material was "sensational happenings in the lives of everyday people." Warner cultivated the belief that such sensational happenings are both symptomatic and representative—symptoms of systemic problems and representative of a host of dramatic events that actually happen to everyday people. MGM proposed that such sensational happenings are accidents and that some accidents are staged by people who are not everyday at all, but undiscovered talents, potential stars, or, as in Stevens's case, producers manqué. J. Phineas Stevens organizes a production unit, not a gang or a union; he makes his money with "cheap, theatrical tricks," not guns or muscle. We can forgive him his faults because, finally, he's entertaining.

The Nuisance belongs to an accident genre that can be tracked in MGM from the late Twenties to the end of the Thirties. It picked up momentum from King Vidor's illustrious *The Crowd*, which pre-

pared the way for prominent MGM features that hinge on accidents which occur in a world without insurance, such as *Captains Courageous, Boys Town,* and, crucially, *The Wizard of Oz,* MGM's first post-New Deal and last major prewar motion picture. *Oz* executes a major shift in the way MGM understood itself and the way it wanted its audience inside and outside the industry to understand it. After the death of boy genius Irving Thalberg in 1938, L. B. Mayer took over production at the studio. Anxious to show the world what he could do, Mayer gave the go-ahead to *The Wizard of Oz,* even though he suspected its massive production budget would squelch profits. *Oz* would prove that MGM, Hollywood's flagship studio, could detach its corporate interests from short-term financial goals. In other words, *Oz* was the product of the same sort of calculations that gave rise to

the big institutional advertising campaigns of other corporations, campaigns which—despite the lack of any data proving such advertising paid for itself with increased profits—had become standard practice because they were thought to raise company morale, increase product recognition among customers, consolidate the power of CEOs over unit managers, and protect the corporation from government interference.

This last had become a critically important consideration by 1939. The palmy days of the corporate liberal concordat had not survived into the second Roosevelt administration. The person the studio imagined itself to be was no longer the soulful corporation eager to cooperate with the feds, but a beleaguered monopoly directly in the sights of Thurman Arnold, head of FDR's Antitrust Division, who threatened a vigorous campaign of prosecutions against the five major movie studios.

The Wizard of Oz responded to Hollywood's antitrust crisis by targeting not one or a set of legal regulations, nor even the social engineering trustbusters, but law and society themselves. There is very little framing narrative in L. Frank Baum's 1905 book, *The Wonderful Wizard of Oz*, and nothing at all about Miss Gulch or Professor Marvel. Baum focuses on a girl, a dog, and a cyclone. If MGM had been Fox, if L. B. Mayer had been Darryl F. Zanuck, and if the screenplay had been written by Nunnally Johnson rather than the MGM writers' colony, Baum's populist allegory—in which the shoes of silver triumph over the bricks of gold—might have been given a Depression updating. Surely the sheriff would have arrived on behalf of the banks or some other grasping capitalist to threaten trouble. But MGM not only discards all traces of Baum's populist economics, it voids economics altogether as a category of concern. *Oz* induces an instant hatred for an unattractive and unpleasant spinster who has been bitten by a dog she was chasing from her garden and who now seeks legal redress. The mortgage is not at stake; nor is the callousness or greed of capitalists at fault: It's a matter of a dog and an order from the sheriff. Furthermore, Miss Gulch's indictment of the dog as a "menace to society" is patently absurd. In close-up Toto looks nothing like Little Caesar. Not only does the dog's cuteness easily outweigh the damage of the unseen bite, but we are automatically more sympathetic to the vividly dramatized affective family of Auntie Em, Uncle Henry, Dorothy, and the hired help than we are to a "society" personified by the horrible and intimidating Miss Gulch. "Society" means as little as "law" to Dorothy, whose response to Miss Gulch's threat is to accept personal responsibility—she volunteers to go to bed without supper—but not liability: the damage to Miss Gulch means nothing to her, nor does the law that the injured woman invokes.

Auntie Em has earlier told Dorothy to "find yourself a place where you won't get into any trouble," and Dorothy has dutifully wished for a trouble-free place "Over the Rainbow." The twister would seem to have fulfilled her wish by depositing her, house, and dog in Oz. But of course Dorothy does get into trouble in Oz, for the twister has dropped her house on a witch. When the Wicked Witch of the West arrives on the scene and wrathfully inquires, "Who killed my sister? Who killed the Wicked Witch of the East, was it you?" Dorothy replies, "No, it was an accident. I didn't mean to kill anybody." Now in Kansas, this might be the prelude to the kind of lawsuit for damages that Miss Gulch had threatened. But while there may be trouble in Oz, there is no law; people can "cause accidents," if not with impunity, at least without threat of damage suits.

MGM was a lot like Oz in that respect. According to author Aljean Harmetz, one of the film's expensive theatrical tricks actually resulted in a gruesome accident to the actress Margaret Hamilton, who played the Wicked Witch of the West. After threatening, "I can cause accidents, too," the Witch was to suddenly disappear in a cloud of smoke and flame. The technicians knew that the shot would be difficult: Hamilton had to move backward to a small trapdoor, and as the elevator descended, both avoid the flames and make sure that her bulky costume would not be caught in the apparatus. After many rehearsals they got the shot; everything worked fine. But the director, Victor Fleming, insisted on a backup shot and an accident did happen. Hamilton got caught in the machinery and suffered first-degree burns over her arm. She left the set and spent the next six weeks in bed, ignoring orders to return to the studio but also rejecting advice from friends to sue, since she knew that no matter how strong her case, should she sue she would never work in Hollywood again. It was MGM's privilege and power, as the dominant company in a company town, to cause accidents with impunity. That is how monopoly works on the ground: It hurts people who are powerless to obtain justice.

Margaret Hamilton's condition of powerlessness was the flip side of the Wicked Witch's conditioned power. The witch can fly through the air on a broom; she can survey the kingdom; she can write orders in the sky; she can dispatch legions of slaves at her command. The Western

Witch appears to have a statelike monopoly on violence in Oz. Yet she cannot cause accidents. That privilege belongs to Dorothy alone. It is by an accident that Dorothy kills the Wicked Witch of the East, and it is by an accident that she bumps off the Wicked Witch of the West. It should be no surprise that a piece of institutional advertising by MGM would have its focal character say, "It was an accident. I didn't mean to kill anybody." That has always been MGM's story, and the studio would stick to it even in the face of Thurman Arnold's charge that monopolies do widespread harm and are a "menace to society."

This emptying out of power and authority in the world of Oz is nowhere clearer than in the Emerald City itself. If the dominion of the Wicked Witch of the West looks like the *Chicago Tribune*'s nightmare version of federal totalitarianism, then the Emerald City looks like the idealization of corporate liberalism—a happy kingdom of various subsidiary companies under the canopy of a corporate headquarters that resembles the "cathedrals of commerce" of lower Manhattan. The corporation seems to work just fine, but it can protect itself from outsiders only by projecting an illusion of wizardry with—not concidentally—the same kind of apparatus and the same special effects that were the stock-in-trade of MGM in the Thirties.

When the Wizard is finally exposed and Oz demystified, we are presented with what looks like a debunking of the "genius" Thalberg legend that would surely gratify Mayer. Except that the bogus wizard is not replaced by another, more authentic wizard. He is replaced by a group of creatures. The pseudo-wizard's departure by balloon thus dramatizes the evacuation of the center of power and tells the corporate fortune of MGM. By recognizing the various virtues of the scarecrow, tin man, and lion, the wizard has acknowledged a new form of mastery: complementary talents organized in a loosely democratic fashion, happily collaborative and adept at improvisation in tight spots—in other words, a team very like the Freed unit, the talent package that would emerge out of the production of *The Wizard of Oz*, dominate the studio's production facilities, define its corporate image during the postwar years, and herald the new mode of independent production that would succeed the studio system. So the allegory does not really work for Thalberg, no matter what Mayer might have wanted the munchkins of Culver City to believe. It was Mayer, not Thalberg who—like the Kansas Wizard—started out in life as a peddler and who bragged about his associations with the "crowned heads of Europe." And if anyone was meant to fly away in a balloon, it was Mayer, a mogul of vast assurances and petty betrayals. In the corporation that MGM had defined itself as being, there was no law to prohibit such usurpation, no insurance against such guile, such finesse. A "kindly philosophy" indeed. 🐝

Cordon Sanitaire

Eric McHenry

Iolanthe

THE best song of the last quarter-century is "Iolanthe" by James McMurtry, but it's a version only I've heard. In the summer of 1995, when McMurtry's album *Where'd You Hide the Body?* was released, I received a promotional cassette copy at the *Topeka Capital-Journal*. I wasn't familiar with James McMurtry—or, for that matter, with his Pulitzer Prize-winning novelist father, Larry—but it was a tape with simply a guy's name on it, and tapes with simply guys' names on them were most of what I was listening to at the time, so I decided to give it a chance. I dropped it into a plastic cassette organizer on the floor of my car and forgot about it.

Then one July day I left all my car's windows rolled up and the organizer on the dashboard. Like a big magnifying glass, the windshield trained the sun on my cassettes and reduced them to a treacly mess. A column describing the accident was probably the best-received piece I ever wrote for the paper:

> I couldn't believe it when I saw it: a big, wavy, bubbly s'more of music. Names and titles were warped but not beyond recognition. The artists formerly known as Bob Dylan, Big Head Todd and Bela Fleck were stuck together—unwilling participants in an improbable supergroup.

The McMurtry tape's case was sufficiently bent that it wouldn't open normally or close completely. The cassette itself looked languid, but for some reason it had sustained little enough internal damage that when I finally played it one day while driving to lunch, it sounded fine. And then it sounded incredible. The first song, "Iolanthe," began with a strange, dragging beat that initially put me off, and McMurtry's voice—parts Lou Reed, David Byrne, and Warren Zevon—was a curiosity. By the time the song was over, though, I knew I would be driving thru. For forty-five minutes I doubled down the same residential streets, rewinding and re-playing it.

The instrumentation was spare in the beginning—an acoustic guitar and that plodding snare beat. But the second-person vocal narrative, with its obsessive a/a/b, c/c/b rhyme pattern, intrigued me:

> Your mother used to take the cure. / She kept plastic on the furniture / in the living room. / You used to tell your friends / if you never saw that place again / it would be too soon. / But your college beau didn't seem so bad. / You brought him home to Mom and Dad / like you're supposed to do. / And he wouldn't account for himself. / And he got along better with the hired help / than he did with you.

And this chorus:

Don't sweat the losses. Let 'em go. / Toss
'em on out where the tall grass grows. /
We're all bound to get our share, / Iolanthe.

McMurtry's delivery was at once racont-
eurish and resigned—and as for resignation,
what about those last two lines? He'd worked
all that time to preserve an unorthodox and
difficult rhyme scheme only to conclude by
chucking it, by deliberately frustrating any ex-
pectation of closure. Ignore the disappointed
rhyme, though, and you're left with words of
familiarity and comfort.

The song continued treading this line between cynicism and solace. Its rhythmic per-
sistence was offset by the growing complex-
ity of its arrangement. The bridge between its
third and fourth verses was a spectacular instrumental confluence, full of swelling and re-
ceding organ and steel guitar. And after the final refrain, just as the song's desultory flour-
ishes were about to overwhelm me, a tuba, for
God's sake, came in with a simple seven-note
progression, repeated it, repeated it again,
cynicism yielded to solace, or in any event
both yielded to the inevitability of moving
on, and the tuba-prodded song went marching away.

I saw an interview with McMurtry in the
"alternative country" magazine *No Depression*,
which was timed roughly to coincide with the
release of his album *It Had to Happen*. Prefacing the conversation, the interviewer provided some background on McMurtry: He as-
serted that *It Had to Happen* was a more fully
realized album than its three predecessors (he
mentioned *Where'd You Hide the Body?* by
name) because McMurtry had finally given
his songwriting some elbow room; he was no
longer hyperextending himself with elaborate
arrangements.

This depressed me because the arrangements I hear on my CD copy of *Where'd You
Hide the Body?*—the arrangements McMurtry

actually presented to the public—sound considerably less elaborate than those on my half-
cooked promotional cassette. The Hammond,
the pedal steel, the harmony and backing vo-
cals, even the tuba and vibraphone (yes,
there's a vibraphone) seem shunted to the far
background. It's possible that McMurtry,
while "mixing" or "mastering" or doing something else removed by several steps from actual performance, opted for an instrumental
paring down because of homogenizing pressure from his folk/country colleagues. The
result was a more austere final draft of *Where'd
You Hide the Body?*, though still too cluttered
for at least one critic.

But I have another theory, and I'm prepared to cling to it against reason. Anyone
with a lab coat can tell you that the world re-
fines itself through arbitrary collision, and
that accidents are the stuff of discovery. Nothing lived, nor was anything dead because
nothing had ever lived, when a lightning bolt
awakened the lake of incipient cells that became our ancestors. We know that we owe the
telephone to a spilled glass of water. I believe
that the intense heat to which I subjected that
cassette was what perfected "Iolanthe's" arrangement. Like a stew whose ingredients can
only be brought into conversation with one
another by hours of stewing, the song, its various instrumental constituents, needed a
chance to simmer. In the CD version, the
pedal steel is an ambulance that never gets
within half a mile of the studio; the tuba is a
basset hound one of the musicians brought,
woofing on the other side of a closed door; the
vibraphone is a series of ideas McMurtry en-
tertains but never mentions. On my cassette,
those instruments were right there in the
room, and they all had the floor.

I wince at those preterites—"were," "had."
The cassette no longer works. It performed
nobly for about a year, but I suspect it had
never fully recovered from its magnifying. The

songs began to sound sluggish. After a while, my car's stereo would mistake the resistance it was feeling for the end of a side and start auto-reversing in perpetuity. At home, my shelf system wouldn't even accept the warped thing. It was the end of "Iolanthe" as I had known it.

The poet August Kleinzahler writes beautifully of irretrievable music:

> Think, this summer forty years ago in Queens,
> Lenny Tristano's quartet was in the Sing Song Room
> of the Confucius Restaurant, playing Mean to Me
> They've played it every night for weeks,
>
> but tonight, when Konitz finishes his solo
> and Lenny digs back in, just then,
> the hair stands up on everyone's neck
> while the bass feeds him lines he tears into bits.
>
> The tape machine is on the blink that set,
> and those two solos, like a million more,
> escape through the exhaust fan and into the night,
> rising along with the car horns and shrieks
>
> until a breeze takes hold and carries them south
> over Brooklyn and the lights of Ebbets Field
> out to Sheepshead Bay and Rockaway Beach,
> swirling awhile then heading off to sea.

Those stanzas belong to a piece generously titled "For Ann, Whose Studio Burnt to the Ground In the Big Futon Factory Fire Across the Freeway From the Coliseum." It opens at twenty thousand feet, where ashes from the cremated paintings have created their own stratum of atmosphere. Kleinzahler offers his Sing Song anecdote as solace to the blighted artist, Ann: her "ellipsoids on canvas" rising to join the musicians' brilliant lost dialogue in darkness and thin air.

All great art is fleeting; transience might be the flaw that stands between the greatest art and perfection. Like Heraclitus's river, it moves on. One person remembers a singular live performance, in which the music seemed to issue from another authority than the musicians. For someone else, a record affords that experience. But it's an early listening, a second or third, when what Philip Larkin called "that hidden freshness" sings clarion, when the tension between familiarity and surprise is tightest, when the song has declared its eloquent theme yet still seems to withhold something vital. That exhilaration can never be revisited, though the record itself might survive another fifty summers. Everyone has a favorite song, and no one hears it more than once.

That's cynicism, of course, but my experience has borne it out. Even before it gave up, the McMurtry cassette was giving me diminishing returns. I played it every day, coursing along Highway 40 on my way to work. And like Highway 40, it ceased to surprise me after a while. Now I loan the CD to friends. I let some time go by between playings. I let myself forget the little instrumental blips, some of the less likely longer passages, the notes McMurtry and his buddies surprised themselves by playing. When I feed it to my finicky shelf system for the first time in a few months, I sometimes find that I've remembered how to listen to it, how not to listen past it. The arrangements always seem understated, incomplete, but the lyrics are no less eloquent than when I heard them for the first time: "We're all bound to get our share." There's the solace.

SUB POP RECORDS AVOIDS TECHNOLOGICAL BARRIERS WITH LP3 FORMAT

Monitor and keyboard intended for display purposes only.

SEATTLE-In a press conference held earlier this afternoon at the Townsville Recreation Center, Sub Pop Records announced their intention to more or less embrace the highly uncontroversial LP3 technology.

In a verbally worded statement to the member of the press in attendance, a Sub Pop spokesperson stated, "We are proud to continue our great tradition of deftly escaping any new scientific breakthroughs and hereby pledge to give our occasional support to LP3."

The LP3 music format has been the focus of little to no debate on the otherwise really exciting Internet. This utter lack of attention has, in part, been due to a concentrated effort by several major record companies to rein the progress of several much more interesting and computer-related music formats. No industry analysts are already predicting the LP3 to be the dominant method of listening to noises in the new millenium.

Although no one is absolutely sure exactly how the LP3

works, some guy I was talking to said that perhaps a magnet or electronic device is used to "read" an encoded message off of a "grooved" "surface". Others claim that the LP3 player, rarely referred to as a spinboard, is little more than an uppity sewing machine.

Despite any claims on the future by the Elders of the Cross, few people agree that with this mild effort Sub Pop Records will be remembered as the leading small to medium sized record company of the 20th Century.

✓	**No download time**
✓	**100% RIAA compliant**
✓	**0MB space required on hard drive**
✓	**Electrically powered**
✓	**Artist livelihood compatible**
✓	**Near CD quality sound**

COME SHRUG AT THE FUTURE WITH OUR NEWEST RELEASES AVAILABLE IN LP3 (OR THE MUCH MORE POPULAR CD FORMATS).

Zen Guerrilla - Trance States In Tongues
(SP 475 LP3/CD)

The Go - Whatcha Doin' (SP 478 LP3/CD)

Love As Laughter - Destination 2000
(SP 490 LP3/CD)

Sub Pop Records. PO Box 20645, Seattle, WA 98102. www. subpop.com

Jack B. Tenney (1891–1970)

JACK Tenney, the man who led the California legislature's famous red-hunting committee, began his career, ironically, as a lawyer whose politics veered from progressive to socialist. Since his views precluded his doing much work with the more profitable type of client, he found himself with a great deal of time on his hands. Like another young attorney of the day named Hoagy Carmichael, Tenney kept himself busy by writing songs. In 1923, capitalizing on a demand for California-related tunes, he composed a ditty called "Mexicali Rose," which was performed by some dance bands of the day and then forgotten.

During the depths of the Depression, Tenney was a supporter of Upton Sinclair's EPIC (End Poverty In California) movement, and was even named as a "subversive" in testimony before the House Un-American Activities Committee in its earliest days in 1938. Soon after that, however, Tenney's politics seemed to change overnight. The shift began with his unsuccessful bid for re-election as president of Local 47, the Los Angeles local of the American Federation of Musicians. Tenney blamed radicals in the L.A. union movement for his defeat, then proceeded to run for the California Assembly as a newly minted anticommunist and was elected. Around the same time, Tenney's songwriting efforts began to pay off when Gene

Autry had a gigantic hit with his version of "Mexicali Rose."

At the start of the assembly's session in 1941, Tenney was selected as chairman of the state's very own committee for investigating political radicals. By the spring of that year, Tenney's committee was calling one "subversive" after another to testify, with particular attention given to Harry Bridges, a chief demon of the redbaiters' universe, and to members of his longshoremen's union in San Francisco.

By the summer of 1941, Tenney began investigating what he termed "red infiltration" of the motion-picture business, issuing subpoenas to several screenwriters, directors, and actors. However, the erstwhile composer did not receive the sort of cooperation from the studios that the famous HUAC hearings would get six years later. Only Walt Disney, convinced that the leaders of the animators' strike at his studio in '41 (including the father of Yo La Tengo's drummer) were fellow travelers at the very least, extended any degree of support to Tenney.

With Pearl Harbor, Tenney abandoned his efforts to Americanize the movies and turned to the "threat" posed by California's Japanese-American population. Throughout the shameful episode that ensued, state and federal officials, sadly including California Attorney General Earl Warren, relied heavily upon the questionable testimony generated by Tenney's committee as they sent Japanese-

Americans off to Manzanar and similar internment camps. In 1944, after becoming a state senator, he investigated the "zoot-suit riots" in Los Angeles—naturally placing the blame on Mexican-American youth.

After the war, as the nation came around to his special kind of inquisition, Tenney resumed his hearings into what he deemed "Red Fascist" labor and motion-picture infiltration, developing a particular animus for dancer Gene Kelly. In 1952 he felt he was ready to be promoted to the bigotry big leagues: the U.S. Congress. His opponent in the Republican primary for the 26th District of California was Jon Holt; Holt's campaign manager was Murray Chotiner, the political guru behind Richard Nixon's various campaigns. In a new book on Nixon, historian Irwin F. Gellman reveals that Chotiner wrote to Nixon asking for the HUAC file that contained information on Tenney's early days as a radical—evidently preparing to red-bait the great red-baiter himself. With considerable misgivings, Nixon sent the file, along with a letter reminding Chotiner that Tenney had reformed himself in the fashion of Whittaker Chambers and that the information in the file was not to be introduced into the campaign. Chotiner did not use the information; Tenney lost in the primary anyway.

Tenney soon began to move in increasingly racist and extremist circles. He appeared on ballots in a number of states that November as the vice-presidential candidate of the Christian Nationalist party. The party's candidate for president, who never accepted its nomination but took no particular steps to keep his name off the party's ballot in the several states in which it appeared, was General Douglas MacArthur. The party's organizer was Gerald L.K. Smith, who was for a decade the country's leading anti-Semite.

Following the elections Tenney began to use his sizable royalties from the many versions of "Mexicali Rose" (still considered a country music standard to this day) to write and publish a stream of books and pamphlets denouncing the "Zionist influence" in American life. With the demise of McCarthyism he left politics to establish a law practice, counting several bigots of regional note among his clients. By the mid-Sixties, his name was appearing on the masthead of *Western Destiny*, one of the era's more rabid journals espousing "Nordic culture." (Among the other notables whose names figured in the masthead were Arthur Ehrhardt, editor of *National Europa*, which featured a number of old Third Reich propagandists among its contributors; Fabrice Laroche, the intellectual mentor of some of the leaders of Jean-Marie Le Pen's movement; and, in one of his early appearances in the annals of extremism, Richard K. Hoskins, whose *White Cycles, Black Cycles* was found in the van of Jewish Community Center attacker Buford O'Neal Furrow.)

Lawrence Dennis (1893–1977)

WHEN Ralph Ellison's posthumous, unfinished novel *Juneteenth* appeared last summer, many reviewers found something quite implausible about the character Bliss, the light-skinned African-American orphan who is informally adopted and raised by a black minister, tours the South as a boy preacher, runs away, and re-emerges as the race-baiting, reactionary U.S. senator from a New England state, Adam Sunraider. Whether or not the forthcoming three-volume edition of Ellison's drafts and manuscripts will establish that he had a real-life model in mind, the fact remains that the writer did not have to search very far in American history to find a man whose career, at least in its early stages, followed this exact trajectory: Lawrence Dennis, the intellectual godfather of American fascism.

In 1897, a couple in Atlanta, classified "mulatto" by the standards of the day, adopted a three-year-old boy and gave him the name Lonnie Lawrence Dennis. Dennis's biological mother was black, so far as the laws of the Peach State were concerned. All that is known of his father is that he was probably white. Lonnie showed an early aptitude for reading and public speaking, and by his fifth birthday he was preaching the Gospel before black congregations in Atlanta. Before long Lonnie, billed as "The Mulatto Boy Evangelist," was touring tent shows from Virginia to Louisiana, appearing at churches across the country and even in England, and speaking before large crowds both white and black. By the age of ten he had written and published his autobiography.

By 1913, Lonnie had long outgrown the role of boy preacher and, no doubt, understood that opportunities of any kind for a "mulatto" in the South were severely circum-scribed. Accordingly, he applied for admission to Phillips Exeter Academy—then as now the most prestigious prep school in America— and was accepted. Though it is unclear whether the school knew of his activities as an evangelist, he apparently was thought to be white when he arrived in New England. Though considered rather reserved and not especially sociable by his classmates, the student now calling himself Lawrence Dennis compiled an outstanding academic record and continued after two years to Harvard, where he became a member of the debate team. After a stint as an officer in France during the First World War, Dennis returned to Harvard, graduated in 1920, and joined the State Department.

Dennis's first posting was to Romania; but after a few months he was sent to Haiti, then occupied by the U.S. Marines but still nominally an independent nation. The abruptness of the change of assignment, and the fact that

Dennis was sent to a "black" nation where nonwhite American diplomatic personnel were then customarily posted, suggests that the State Department initially assumed he was white but subsequently learned of his background. From Haiti he was sent to Honduras (also a nation with a substantial black population) and then became chargé d'affaires in Nicaragua (which also has a number of immigrants from the West Indies). In 1926, he found himself in the crossfire, literally and figuratively, between insurgents supporting Augusto Sandino (from whose name "Sandinista" derives) and a coalition of U.S. business interests and their local compradors. Following the arrival of the Marines and the loss of a hundred American and three thousand Nicaraguan lives, Dennis negotiated a settlement between the factions that satisfied American corporate interests in the region and kept Sandino on the defensive until he was killed in 1935. Disgusted by his part in enforcing the Monroe Doctrine, Dennis publicly denounced the settlement in June 1927 and resigned from the State Department. For several years he worked in Peru as a banker for the New York-based house of J. and W. Seligman, in which capacity he offered his views on the advisability of loans to Latin American governments (he usually opposed them). In April 1930, six months after the stock market crash, he resigned his banker's job, settled in New York, and began work as a social critic.

In November and December 1930, Dennis's series in The New Republic, "Sold On Foreign Bonds," a scathing critique of investment banking, caused a sensation with its combination of cool analysis and acid wit, elements which continued to distinguish Dennis's writing through nearly all the twists and turns of his career. In early 1931, he published a well-argued critique of American intervention in Central America in Foreign Affairs. By that time he had been offered a book contract, and Dennis set to work on his first book, Is Capitalism Doomed?

This volume, the only book of Dennis's never subsequently republished by his extremist admirers, appeared in 1932 and was well received, especially on the left; Norman Thomas gave it a thoughtful review in The Nation, and the next year John Strachey, in the bestselling Marxist tract The Coming Struggle For Power, commented that "Mr. Dennis has written a far more penetrating analysis of the crises [of the Depression] than has been achieved by any professional capitalist economist."

Dennis's argument, simply put, was that for thirty years or more Americans had been unable to accept the closing of the frontier, and that our use of Latin American and Asian nations as economic fiefdoms was an attempt to feed an expansionist economy that, as recent events showed, was doomed to contract. It was Dennis's view that Americans should, first of all, lower their economic expectations. To put the Depression behind it, Dennis argued, the United States had to abandon economic intervention in other lands, close its borders to imports and forget about exports, impose heavy taxation on large fortunes, and use the revenues to administer relief to the middle classes. The government should discourage expansion and mechanization of American agriculture, end the tendency toward conglomeration in business, and reinstate the Jeffersonian vision of the United States as a predominantly agricultural, self-sufficient nation.

Although his ideas were seen as impractical, Dennis was prominent enough in those years to be invited to testify before Ferdinand Pecora's famous Senate committee inquiring into the causes of the Depression. The improvisational nature of the first Roosevelt administration, though, convinced him that democratic institutions, while capable of averting disaster in the short term, were too weak to bring about recovery in the long term. Before long Dennis was flirting with the most alarming sort of authoritarianism. A letter of April 15, 1933 gives an idea of his state of mind at the time and, in a way, foretells his future:

> In times of prosperity when there is a great demand for all kinds of services, people like me find places without seeking. But, when the competition becomes keen, things become impossible for us. Mind you, I am not whining. I am a fatalist. I am prepared to take my medicine in the bread line, the foreign legion or with a pistol shot in the mouth, and I ask no sympathy and would resent an indication of pity just as I would have neither sympathy nor mercy on thousands of people now in the seats of the mighty if I came to power. I should like nothing better than to be a leader or follower of a Hitler who would crush and destroy many now in power. It is my turn or fate now to suffer. It may someday be theirs. I am too intelligent or intellectual to believe it is anyone's fault. This mechanistic philosophy saves me from a sense of inferiority, guilt, or personal failure.

In the years to come, Dennis wrote of his neo-Jeffersonian ideals in more theoretical terms and came around more and more to the idea of a strong leader who would utilize the capitalist class instead of eliminating it—what he characterized as the "authoritarian executive state," or, in a word, fascism.

By late 1933, he was associate editor of *The Awakener,* a publication edited by the notorious anti-Semite Joseph P. Kamp and which had ties with the Nazis and Mussolini's government. Dennis began work on another book, *The Coming American Fascism,* and sometimes spoke of becoming a right-hand man to an American Duce or Führer; he would sometimes compare this advisory role

to a Göbbels, sometimes to a Harry Hopkins. His handful of collegiate and intellectual followers, including budding architect Philip Johnson, were puzzled as to why Dennis, a commanding speaker and debater who held his own in panel discussions, was reluctant to become a leader himself; they knew nothing of his days as Lonnie Dennis.

In late 1934, with Dennis's encouragement, Philip Johnson and another follower, Alan Blackburn of the Museum of Modern Art, traveled to Louisiana to sound out Huey Long about joining forces; Long, uninterested, declined to work with Dennis. In 1935, Dennis left *The Awakener* and joined E.A. Pierce and Co., a New York brokerage firm, as an economist. The next year, *The Coming American Fascism* was issued, and Dennis began contributing a series of articles to *The American Mercury* at the invitation of editor Paul Palmer, with titles such as "The Highly Moral Causes Of War" and "Liberalism Commits Suicide." He became a fixture at Park Avenue dinner parties; Matthew Josephson, in his autobiography, mentions an exchange at one of them. Dennis, asked to expostulate on his social theories, was outlining to a spellbound table his vision of revolution, complete with fascisti mercilessly lining up leftists against the wall. A freshly minted graduate from one of the Eastern colleges interrupted him: "Mr. Dennis, I have to tell you that I attend Communist Party meetings, so I suppose you'll have to shoot *me* when you come to power." Dennis's expression shifted instantly from the stern gaze of the zealot to amusement: "Shoot *you,* ma'am? Why, I'll do no such thing—I'll give you a job!"

With such repartee and argument—combined with some skill at predicting the fluctuations of a market slowly climbing out of the Depression—Dennis, now commonly referred to as "the intellectual leader of American fascism," began to assemble an audience for his writings, some of whom were well-heeled enough to shell out $24 a year for a weekly newsletter featuring his comments on world events and investment advice. Accordingly, he left E. A. Pierce in 1938 and began to publish the *Weekly Foreign Letter*. If he avoided anti-Semitism in the *Letter*, he made it clear that he considered Hitler's regime to be a permanent part of the world scene, and warned against U.S. involvement in European affairs. Joining England and the Soviet Union in war against the Nazis, he reasoned, would simply deliver Germany and perhaps all of Europe to the Communists, while the strain of war would leave America open to fascist invasion and waste lives and materiel. It would be much better, he argued, if America simply moved in a fascist direction on its own and avoided the European war altogether.

The principals of the Third Reich were highly appreciative of Dennis's thinking and warmly welcomed him when he visited Berlin with an E. A. Pierce partner in July 1936. Details of this visit are given in *The Official German Report*, a book prepared in 1946 by O. John Rogge, an assistant attorney general investigating American contact with the Nazis. Rogge recounts a conversation between Dennis and the "philosopher" of the Nazi movement, Alfred Rosenberg. The American asked the Nazi leader: "Why don't you treat the Jews more or less as we treat the Negroes in America?" That is to say, perhaps: *Instead of modifying the law to strip them of all their rights as citizens, why not modify it to guarantee them all the rights of citizens, and then enact upon that a mountain of regulations and rules, and selective enforcement of laws, making the rights conferred worse than meaningless?* Dennis's next suggestion, indeed, supports this interpretation: "You can practice discrimination and all that, but be a little hypocritical and moderate and don't get in conflict with American opinion." Rogge doesn't give

Rosenberg's reply, but years later Dennis reported that it was that such a course of action would be *nicht anständig*, a rough translation of which would be somewhere between "disgraceful" and "dishonorable."

As war clouds gathered, Dennis's articles and public appearances became more frequent: In January 1941, he participated in a debate sponsored by *The Nation* on the question of U.S. intervention in the war. He began to spend time with some of the leaders of the America First movement, including Charles and Anne Morrow Lindbergh. In 1940 Harper printed Dennis's third book, *The Dynamics of War and Revolution*, but after protests from a number of the firm's authors who supported the Allied cause, publication was canceled and the sheets were turned over to Dennis, who bound and distributed them himself. "I do not believe in democracy or the intelligence of the masses," Dennis wrote.

> Contrary to the apparent belief of the Republican Party sponsors of reactionary stooges, no political movement anywhere today can long succeed as the ostensible cause of the rich versus the poor. Hitler was able to exploit with guile the gullibility of the "best" people, and with the utmost sincerity the patriotism of the nationalists who wanted to see Versailles avenged. The anticommunist line got the capitalists, the anti-Versailles line got the army and the nationalists, and the anti-Semitic line got the masses as well as the classes, while, at the same time, sugarcoating the initial pill of anticapitalism.

Though Dennis's third book had its share of reviewers (such as Karl Korsch in *Partisan Review*) who noted his skill at argument but disputed his conclusions, he was clearly on a collision course with the Roosevelt administration. Secretary of the Interior Harold Ickes denounced him as an "appeaser" in a speech. At the same time, subscriptions to the *Weekly*

Foreign Letter began dropping, the FBI began surveillance of Dennis, and his sources of income became increasingly shadowy. Though Dennis kept some distance from the activities of the German-American Bund, he was in touch with German diplomats through George Sylvester Viereck, and Rogge notes that during 1940 and 1941 Dennis received up to $12,000, some of which seems to have come from various German newspapers. During this time, he also began receiving money for piecemeal editorial work from *Reader's Digest*, where his old friend Paul Palmer was an editor.

With the bombing of Pearl Harbor, Dennis promptly offered his services to the Armed Forces. The army refused him a commission, though, and from this point Dennis was practically treated as an enemy agent. The postmaster general barred distribution of the *Weekly Foreign Letter* in the mails, and Dennis ceased publication of the newsletter in June 1942. By this time he was receiving $400 a month from *Reader's Digest* via a public relations firm, in exchange for which he read and condensed various articles. In the fall of 1942 he was visited by the investigative reporter John Roy Carlson disguised as a sympathetic fascist, and Dennis proceeded to offer his usual barbed opinions about American democracy: pondering whether Lindbergh or perhaps the ultra-reactionary General George Van Horn Moseley might be able to run America "with a circle of nationalistic advisors"; predicting that America would go fascist in the process of fighting fascism; and forecasting that a wave of anti-Semitism would usher in such a process. When Carlson quoted Dennis at length in *Under Cover*, the dramatic exposé of the American far right that was among the top nonfiction bestsellers of 1943, Dennis came under a barrage of attacks in newspapers and radio.

In his book, Carlson commented: "Born in

Atlanta, 'of a long line of American ancestors,' Dennis's hair is woolly, dark and kinky. The texture of his skin is unusually dark and the eyes of Hitler's intellectual keynoter of 'Aryanism' [a word in none of Dennis's books, it should be noted] are a rich, deep brown, his lips fleshy." Lest the reader miss Carlson's point, Walter Winchell informed his millions of listeners that Dennis, the putative champion of white power, was in fact of "mixed" parentage. Dennis did not reply to this "revelation," and on those occasions in future decades when he spoke of race relations he made no reference to his being of a particular race.

After being passed over in the July 1942 and January 1943 mass indictments for sedition, Dennis was finally charged in the third and final indictment. His case went to trial in April 1944, and Dennis defended himself on civil liberties grounds. After five months of proceedings, the presiding judge died of a heart attack and a mistrial was declared.

Dennis lived quietly in New York until the end of the war. In March 1946, he resumed publication of his weekly newsletter, whose 400 or 500 subscribers, paying $24 a year apiece, provided his income for the next two decades. The subscribers, according to Dennis's mailing list, included the likes of Herbert Hoover, Burton Wheeler, Amos Pinchot, and Bruce Barton, adman and author of *The Man Nobody Knows*. In one of his impish moods, Dennis gave the revived newsletter the title of the old Socialist paper, *Appeal To Reason*.

Week by week, in the *Appeal*'s five mimeographed pages, Dennis presented arguments very much in keeping with his earliest writings: that most foreign aid did nothing to benefit the recipient and unfairly enriched the nation offering "assistance"; that Communism was not the path for America to take, but that it was not America's business to contain it abroad or to endlessly search for its influ-

ence at home; that the United States should get out of Latin America and leave its neighbors in peace. As Ronald Radosh observed (back in the days when he was the bright hope of the William Appleman Williams school of revisionist historians), Dennis frequently anticipated the concerns of the American left of the Sixties. He was highly critical of the McCarthy investigations, frequently comparing the techniques employed in them to those of the sedition trial in which he had been a defendant. When McCarthy died, he offered an obituary with his old sardonic touch, calling "Tailgunner Joe" a "typical, sincere, roof-raising American—a most authentic type, who never quite grasped that sin is here to stay and has to be lived with."

His days as a menace to American democracy long past, Dennis contributed an interview to Columbia's oral-history program in the early Sixties. In late 1969, he published his last book, *Operational Thinking For Survival*, with the small Denver house of Ralph Myles, which specialized in isolationist volumes. Frederick Schuman, Dennis's leftist debating partner from three decades earlier and a target of McCarthy's hearings, reviewed the new volume in *The Nation,* asserting that Dennis, for all his sinister reputation, still had something to say to America.

But by now Dennis was running out of energy. His newsletter ceased to appear in 1972. Not long afterward he moved up to Spring Valley, New York to be near one of his two daughters, who had married the man who ran Pink Floyd's light show in the late Sixties. Dennis died in August 1977—a man whose solutions to American problems, as expressed in his writings, are unacceptable to anyone who believes in democracy, but whose analysis of those problems reverberates in a fashion, that, while uncomfortable, is serious enough to deserve attention.   🖎

A Semi-permissive Environment

My model personality
Slams into the side of a bus
Trained to obliterate or hide
He was suspect of the mother
& father; could move a whole
Madness while banking on good
Relations. At shutter speed
Not a soul notices candor
Becoming manipulation
I contain multitudes
Sanctioning slaughter
The blood pressure swells
With mixed emotions
In an infrastructure's gutter
We've a treaty alliance
To rectify your internal strife

—Anselm Berrigan

LONE GUNMAN THEORY

PAUL MALISZEWSKI

I.

ONE cubicle away, my managing editor was on the telephone trying to reach a prospective freelance writer who had materialized out of the vast wasteland of New York's north country. "I need a number for Noah Warren-Mann," he told an operator. A query letter had arrived from Noah recently, bearing story ideas aplenty, and my managing editor was apparently eager to speak with the man whose e-mail messages, rich in parentheticals and exclamation points, conveyed a passion for business and an aspiration to join the team. ("That's Warren *hyphen* Mann.") I knew a bit about Noah. ("Could you look under 'Mann' too?") I knew he had no phone, for instance, and that every wildcard search would come up empty. ("You checked Felt Mills *and* Watertown?") I knew this because Noah Warren-Mann was I.

My career as a hack journalist for the *Business Journal* of Central New York developed alongside a satiric project in which I invented personae of various rhetorical stripes and covertly authored a series of increasingly cranky and, I thought, increasingly preposterous letters to the editor. The newspaper published each one as fact. Besides Noah, I manufactured nine other characters, many of whom I wrote about in these pages ("I, Faker," BAFFLER No. 11). While I gleaned not a little satisfaction from creating a fictional universe to send

up not only my own reporting but also the newspaper's twice-monthly menu of thuggish conservatism, still I felt something was missing. In order to really satirize the vacuity of business journalism I needed to infect the news pages.

Enter Noah Warren-Mann. Born and bred in humble Watertown, New York, this up-and-coming young businessman dreamed of the high-tech, gadget-galore life he had read about in *Wired* and *Fast Company*, and was committed to achieving it in his hometown, a city known, if at all, as the birthplace of the ubiquitous pine tree-shaped air freshener. While Noah had what high school guidance counselors charitably call "potential" and "enthusiasm," his best efforts produced MicroVisions, a one-man computer maintenance company that fit comfortably in the trunk of a small car. True, Watertown barely sustained Noah's most micro of visions and, true, he didn't have a telephone, but the newspaper held him in high regard anyway and published his first article, "Upstate Businesses Recover Slowly from Wicked Ice Storm." Only the ice storm was real.

After paying his dues with such mundane reporting, the stage was set for Noah's star turn. He would profile Teloperators Rex, Inc., a homegrown company with the revolutionary idea of using people to answer telephones. After a number of editorial delays, which had nothing to do with the story's utter lack of veracity, "T.R.I. Brings On-Call

Phone Personnel to the North Country" ran in the June 8, 1998 issue of the *Business Journal*. The headline stretched across the top of two inside pages.

The published article delivered exciting glimpses of the habits and musings of TRI's principal, one Irving T. Fuller. In tones of breathless awe, Noah described the owner's lifelong but utterly irrelevant fascination with dinosaurs and, like any good profiler, used detail to offer tinker-toy psychological insights into his entrepreneurial epiphany (a young Irv standing before a *T. Rex*) and resulting character:

> Today, there are large framed prints of a triceratops, an archaeopteryx, and a delta-dromeus on the walls of Fuller's office in Watertown, along with movie posters from *Jurassic Park* and *The Lost World*. On an antique mahogany credenza behind him, pictures of his wife and three children share space with a close-up photo of a stegosaurus skull and an artist's rendering of a brachiosaurus—a slow, gentle-seeming herbivore in muted pastel tones. A cleverly painted plaster cast of a thighbone sits propped up against the back wall of his office, flanking a large picture window on one side, with the U.S. flag on the other. The bone easily stands floor to ceiling, with one panel of the acoustic drop ceiling moved aside so that it continues on up into the wiring and the dark. The replica, he says, was cast in a limited edition from the Rex held by the Museum of Natural History, the very skeleton that long ago fired Fuller's imagination.

Naturally Noah was as eager to explain Fuller's "Darwinian" philosophy of management as he was to tell us about his phone-answering system: "A recent memo to inspire the marketing staff began, 'First, let's cogitate like the advanced primates we supposedly are. Personally, I gave up thinking like a lizard, and

you should, too.'" We counted ourselves lucky to sit at the feet of this impressive thinker and merely collect his pearls:

> "Evolution is not, as some people believe, about the changes occurring in organisms due to adaptation, natural selection, and other forces that are so minute and gradual as to be not directly observable given their long-term nature. It's really about not missing the next big thing. It's about adapting yourself and modeling yourself and rigorously remaking yourself quickly enough in order to embody the next big thing before it's even big. Evolution is about electing to survive."

"Fuller" was so pleased with Noah's bouquet that he decided to excerpt it on the company's Web site. He also created a media kit around the glowing profile and, in the hope of reaching a broader audience, sent it to journalists at local television stations and daily newspapers.

Web sites, as we all know, are crucial to reaching that anonymous, broader audience. TRI's site (which a later news article described as "very professional") was in fact designed and placed on-line in a single night by my brother. We spent no money and settled on a simple aesthetic: Appropriate and cobble together the gaudy dreck of non-fictional corporate Web pages. Like medieval alchemists, we sought to transmute their crap into TRI's gold plating. A pseudo-Celtic symbol, chosen more for its size than any particular meaning, became the perfect corporate logo for a company declaring itself "Your choice for the new millennium." AT&T's and MCI's Web sites coughed up all manner of generic images of telephones and operators. Stock photographs used to gussy up especially thin year-end reports did wonders for TRI's image. An animated Hewlett-Packard banner ad, after a little doctoring, crowed about TRI's Vetracom

2000: "Simply . . . let us answer your telephone." The Web site showcased non-news (Look, new Web site!) and the trophies of a year's invented successes (opportunities in Europe and an economic development grant courtesy of Governor Pataki). All very professional, indeed.

I didn't really expect local journalists, once they received the media kit, which included Noah's profile and a sheaf of press releases, to perpetuate the TRI hoax. I figured its days were numbered. Readers in Watertown had, after all, informed the *Business Journal* just days after Noah's article ran that there was no Fuller, no TRI, no Noah, anywhere. What I did expect is that people would look at the Web site, the stack of fake press releases, the profile, and realize, without my prompting, that TRI—which clearly doesn't exist—was a lot like other businesses, with their own very professional Web sites, press releases, and hagiographic profiles. That this, to put it simply, was a satire.

And, indeed, the reporters who contacted TRI by e-mail were definitely wandering in the country of humor. "Congratulations," a reporter in Syracuse wrote. "It was a fun read." Another, based in Albany, enthused: "Your George E. Pataki press release was dead on. Most of it reads exactly the same way the stuff from the gov's office does. . . . Also, I must tell you, the governor's chief press spokesman is not amused."

Within three days of being mailed, the media kits generated articles in the *Syracuse Post-Standard* and the *Watertown Daily Times*, and WSTM-TV3 ran a story about TRI in both of its evening newscasts.[†] But instead of grasping the satire, as I'd hoped they would,

the reporters focused on TRI as a Byzantine flimflam. Setting the tone of the coverage, each article quoted the governor's press secretary, who said, "This falls into the realm of the bizarre"—adding in one account, "It's clearly inappropriate." Eager to lend seriousness to the story, both articles also raised the specter of a government investigation, with the Watertown newspaper suggesting that TRI's media kit provoked widespread panic: "The counterfeit press release had gubernatorial and legislative press aides scrambling to figure out what was going on, and Attorney General Dennis C. Vacco's office is now investigating." State officials did not speculate about TRI's motives, but the *Business Journal's* managing editor plied local reporters with suggestions of "some kind of elaborate business scam at the heart" of the hoax.

The real scam was the way reporters spun press releases into news. I was pleased to note how the reporters lifted my own strategic phrasings. The Syracuse story—about 40 percent of which was taken word for word from the media kit—concluded with three lengthy quotations from my fake press releases, my Governor Pataki, and my state senator.

II.

AFTER a few days and a few articles, the story of TRI expired, the failed yet perplexing swindle of a north country confidence man. Meanwhile, a new misunderstanding was taking shape. It turned out I *was* being investigated. On September 23, 1998, two agents from the state attorney general's office visited me at work (I'd left the *Business Journal* for another job in February) and questioned me

---

[†] Contrary to the headlines and reporting in the Watertown and Syracuse newspapers ("Faux Fax Creates Scramble, Query" and "Fax Too Good to be True" respectively), I sent no fax. Someone, perhaps at a state agency, perhaps an editor or reporter, took distribution into his own hands. Both writers very likely reported on the effects of the media's subsequent, wider circulation of my humbly mailed media kit.

for the better part of two hours about TRI and a press release bearing an uncanny resemblance to those issued by Governor Pataki. "Can I call you Paul or should I call you Noah?" asked the senior member of the duo. My impression was that he had thought of this line at least twenty-four hours earlier.

The investigators were very serious men. They told me I was looking at possible charges on multiple counts of criminal forgery and some vaguely defined "computer crimes." They gestured ominously and with noticeable pride to two stuffed accordion folders labeled "Press Release." My bogus publicity circular, just more than a page, had blossomed into their evidence. It looked like the consequence of being misunderstood was being arrested. If I really had awakened in the land of the literally minded, then I wanted to be perfectly clear.

So I explained my project, much as I have in these essays, as a satire. The officers didn't exactly warm to my apologia. The junior investigator was particularly skeptical, repeatedly scolding me. He called my project "selfish," the cause of a costly government investigation, and said that what I'd done was like "the guy who sees a weakness in the security of the bank and so robs the bank to prove it can be done instead of using your gifts and intelligence to fix the problem in a straightforward manner." But I persisted. To their insinuations that I was a forger and even insane, I talked about satire and the use of literary pseudonyms. At last, the skeptic asked, "But doesn't satire require that people recognize it as satire?" I took it less as a follow-up question than a signal that, finally, I was being understood.

Then the investigators asked me to commit myself—on paper. I was to provide a statement about my project—and nothing clever this time. I told them I'd think about what I wanted to say and type something up. "Look,

we're not asking you to go off and make some kind of literary creation," the skeptic shot back. "We want you to sit here and write, by hand, what you did and why." And so I explained it all again, filling several pages with short, unmodified declarative sentences. I larded the statement so heavily with keywords such as "literary," "satire," and "fictional project" that even a devotee of *Ally McBeal* could see that underneath their charges of forgery broiled a First Amendment case, with all the attendant media scrutiny and bad publicity that implies.

While I wrote, the officers got down to business with their cell phones. One of them received a call for his partner. Their phones were identical; it seemed they'd accidentally been switched. When I finished writing, the senior officer notarized, signed, and initialed the sheets and had his partner fax them to an attorney. We waited awhile. Then we left my office and went to theirs and waited some more. The attorney, I learned, was to evaluate my written statement, consider the relevant legal statutes, and decide what crimes to have me arrested for. I would be arrested that day, the skeptic assured me. The only question was on what charges.

I found it difficult to eat my lunch. I couldn't imagine keeping my sandwich down. I bit at an apple and polished off my water. We waited some more. Finally, word came back that the attorney did not wish to press charges or make an arrest at this time. At what time would the attorney wish to press charges? I asked. The officers couldn't say. They were going to continue their investigation, they said. I asked when they planned on winding this up. Again, they couldn't say for sure. The senior investigator said: "It may be two weeks or it may be two months. The longer it is, the better off you are."

Before saying goodbye, the skeptic had some final advice for me, which I dutifully pass along to aspiring Swifts out there: "If you want to be a satirist, get a pen and a pad of paper, write something, and then publish it conventionally. If I open the paper one day and see you're on the *New York Times* bestseller list, then I'll know you're a real satirist."

Despairing of ever living up to the officer's standards and becoming a real writer, I hastily looked to tie up loose narrative threads and conclude my fakes project.

III.

IN MID-AUGUST the *Business Journal* had apologized belatedly for the publication of Noah's TRI article, printing "We Apologize," an unsigned notice that was a study in complex obfuscation.

> For twelve years the *Business Journal* has prided itself on providing the Central New York business community with accurate and useful information, information that our readers rely on to keep them informed about businesses and issues in our region.

> On June 8, we fell victim to what now appears to be a hoax, in publishing a free-lancer's profile of a relatively young company in the Watertown area.

The apology mentioned only a single fake article and not by name—or should I say, *what now appears to be* a fake article. The paper (read: victim) also knew Noah's other article was a fake, and besides that had published sixteen letters to the editor and business columns that were (unbeknownst to its editors) fake as well.

> A subsequent phone call from a well-informed reader in Watertown sparked our initial suspicions about the story, so we immediately began investigating to determine

whether the story was truth or fiction. Despite repeated attempts, we have been unable to make contact with the principals in the firm.

One would, the apology suggested, have to be a well-informed reader in Watertown to spot the fakery, as if advanced knowledge were necessary, including, perhaps, a proficiency with foreign languages and the ability to converse with natives.

> We were continuing our efforts to resolve our questions about the article when we received a mailing from the supposed company on August 3. The mailing included a news release that appeared to be from Governor George Pataki's office and announced that the company had received more than $1 million in state economic development grants. We immediately contacted the state's economic-development arm, Empire State Development Corp., to inform officials about the release. In fact, it was the *Business Journal*'s call that alerted state officials to the apparent escalation of the hoax.

First the victim of a hoax, then the hero of the day? Apparently this was an apology with a happy ending.

> We regret that we originally published an article that appears to be a fabrication. The *Business Journal* prizes its reputation for credibility with our readers and strives always to meet or exceed their expectations.

What appears to be the *Business Journal*'s apology was not the last word on the fakes. Later I saw the newspaper's editorial/opinion page step boldly into the breach, weighing in several times on the "issue" of fakery and journalism scandals, though always neglecting to mention the paper's close acquaintance with both. In his January 15, 1999 call to arms, publisher Norman Poltenson blamed journalism scandals on a loose industry not subject to press scrutiny, overrun with people of "a decidedly left-wing slant" and reporters who are "crusaders, out to change society." Three months later the paper's ersatz media critic could only offer thin, homiletic gruel such as "Don't believe anything you hear and only half of what you see"—sternly concluding, "Let the viewer beware!"

But these implicit responses to the apology were preceded by another. Gary Pike, one of my earliest fictional personae, a man of strong opinions, a conservative's conservative, who had last written in with a bit of impressionistic babble about the future of shopping malls, was first to accept the paper's apology.

"Apology Accepted," the *Business Journal*, September 28, 1998

To the Editor:

I write to congratulate the *Business Journal* for having the editorial guts and wherewithal to stand up and apologize to its readers ("We Apologize," August 17, 1998, p. 3). The fact that you are a) able and b) willing to apologize in a straight-forward and honest manner, admitting that "what now appears to be a hoax" was published in the newspaper, speaks volumes for you and the kind of work you do. I have no idea to what article you refer, but I nevertheless applaud you for having the integrity to tell us the complete story—you were a victim of another's deceit—and come clean about your minor mistake.

In a year in which many mistakes were made in the name of journalism, from Stephen Glass at *The New Republic* to the African-American poet/columnist Patricia Smith and the great Mike Barnicle at the *Boston Globe* to the unnecessary investigation of the corporate practices of the Chiquita Banana Company by a muck-raking troublemaker at the *Cincinnati Enquirer*, your inci-

dent stands out as being minor and your apology magnanimous. I cannot, of course, speak for all your readers, but, as for this reader, apology accepted. . . .

On the same day I read your apology, I later heard President Clinton attempt to apologize to the American people. The two apologies sat down side by side in my mind for the next few days—yours an example of how to do it right and the other a textbook example of extreme disingenuousness and dubious logic. Anyone who tuned in and saw *The Bill Clinton Show* on TV will agree that copping to "a relationship that was inappropriate; in fact, it was wrong" is a far cry from what you say in fewer words and with no misdirection whatsoever. If only our nation's Commander-in-Chief could have taken a hint from your pages and spoken with one-half the percentage of clarity that permeates through your sentences, as in the following: "We regret that we originally published an article that appears to be a fabrication."

In conclusion, what most cheers me is learning that you investigate yourselves. This reader's mind is put at ease knowing that you investigated the article after publishing it and maintained your efforts even as the principals in the firm apparently aimed to foist their apparent deception on unsuspecting victims. Let it escape nobody's attention, therefore, that it was only because of this newspaper's being literally on the ball that state officials were alerted to the hoax's "apparent escalation." I, for one, can rest easily knowing that you are watching the news and watching yourselves watch the news, acting as both guardian of journalism's lighted torch of truth and the watchdog guarding against journalism's occasional mistakes. Once more, my hat is off to you, my head bowed, and pate exposed.

Gary Pike, Syracuse, N.Y.

ATLAS FINALLY SHRUGGED

Us Against Them in the Me Decade

Christian Parenti

Rising unemployment was a very desirable way of reducing the strength of the working classes. . . . What was engineered—in Marxist terms—was a crisis in capitalism which re-created a reserve army of labor, and has allowed the capitalists to make high profits ever since.
—Alan Budd, chief economic adviser to Margaret Thatcher, 1992

THE LATE Sixties and early Seventies were a tough time for the owners of American industry. The postwar recovery had peaked. Europe and Japan had rebuilt their industries and transformed themselves from hungry markets for American goods and capital into aggressive economic rivals. Newly industrializing countries, too, were joining the game. After more than two decades of virtually uninterrupted growth there was just too much stuff circulating the planet. Too many cars, too many shoes, too many refrigerators and not enough people with money to absorb the abundance. Anyone who could afford such things pretty much already had them by the mid-Sixties and that spelled disaster. It was a classic formula: Too much success glutted markets and shrank profits.

To complicate matters, mass rebellion, particularly of the socialist and Third World nationalist sort, was breaking out around the globe. As the United States continued to lose badly in Vietnam (and not for lack of lethal effort), the American political establishment—liberals and conservatives alike—lost credibility. The civil rights movement and peaceful antiwar rallies on campus had given way to massive urban riots and homegrown "terrorism." By the war's end even American GIs were a liability, on occasion casting their antiwar vote via hand grenades. In 1970 alone the military, which preferred to suppress news of dissent, gave an official "fragging count" of 363.

And where was labor in this political maelstrom? Where was the mainstream American working class, that supposed host of somnambulant Archie Bunkers? They sent their boys to die in Nam, grieved quietly by themselves, and, as the official image informs us, donned their hardhats for the occasional prowar, flag-waving Nixon rally, right? Actually, the real saga of labor during those troubled years is one of disobedience, chaos, "counterplanning," malingering, and huge, militant wildcat strikes. It was in response to this crisis—a crisis of excess democracy and excess working-class power—and the vicissitudes of overproduction that the great right-wing backlash of the last three decades was born. To understand what happened next it is crucial to understand that for the first time since the Depression the American business class felt its back pressed against the wall.

The Sleeping Giant Stirs

LABOR's "new mood" first made headlines in 1968, the year political revolt broke out around the world. The United Farm Workers were gaining national attention and winning contracts. Walter Reuther, president of the behemoth United Auto Workers, was taking an increasingly progressive stance against racism, the war in Vietnam, and the AFL-CIO's pampered, pussyfooting leaders. In May 1968 AFL-CIO President George Meany suspended the UAW from the federation. A little more than a month later Reuther withdrew his 1.5 million members and with the Teamsters, the country's largest union, formed the Alliance for Labor Action. All the while, the UAW was bringing home the bacon, having just beaten Ford in a two-month strike.

Around the same time public-sector workers—who by and large did not have the right to strike—began to agitate. In February 1968, New York sanitation workers, ignoring the law and threats of jail, walked out and left the city's refuse to mount in frozen, rat-infested heaps for nine days. Mayor John V. Lindsay called the strike "blackmail" and refused to give

in to workers' demands, until the more sober Governor Nelson Rockefeller overruled him, capitulated, and boosted wages for the garbagemen. But their strike had become a spectacle of national proportions. Soon followed word of the American Federation of Teachers' drive to collect a million-dollar "militancy fund" as teachers staged small but widespread illegal strikes in Maryland, Florida, and New Mexico. A fretful *U.S. News & World Report* noted "a new, aggressive mood among public employees."

Strikes hobbled American industry in the first four months of 1968 to an extent they hadn't since 1950, and in most disputes labor emerged victorious. By late June federal mediators were involved in 353 strikes, which had idled 219,000 workers in trades ranging from construction to journalism. In Detroit, for example, workers shut down both the city's papers for seven and a half months, while the building trades brought the construction industry to its knees for most of the summer. Labor was only beginning to feel its strength.

Nineteen sixty-nine brought the first of several truly titanic showdowns. In October General Electric faced off against a coalition of twelve unions. Since the Forties GE had been known as one of the most antiunion corporations in America. Its take-it-or-leave-it approach to contract negotiation and its ruthless cost-cutting went by the moniker "Boulwarism" in honor of the company's notorious personnel manager, Lemuel Boulware. The company's heavy hand was of no avail in the strike of 1969–70, when workers shut hundreds of GE plants from Burlington, Vermont to Oakland, California. With

ON THE STICK

DAVID MOBERG

If Hollywood were casting *Backlash: Attack from the Right*, the male lead would probably be a white guy—call him "Butch"—with a short haircut and a vaguely Southern accent. His Ford pickup truck would have a gun rack and bumper stickers announcing "Abortion Kills" and "Born Again." His radio would be tuned to Rush Limbaugh. But the movie could be cast differently. Butch could be "Brad," an altogether different white guy, corporate counsel for a large manufacturer, riding home from work in his Lincoln Navigator, his radio tuned to NPR's *Marketplace* as he talks on his cell phone about the day's business: busting a union organizing drive, shifting a factory from Warren, Ohio to Ciudad Juarez, and subcontracting as much janitorial and clerical work as possible—while cutting pension and health care benefits for the workers who remain on the payroll.

In the popular imagination, the conservative ascendancy of the last two decades is one part reality check on postwar liberalism, one part cultural backlash against the excesses of the Sixties New Left. The

133,000 strikers coast to coast walking pickets, production at the nation's fourth largest employer ground to a halt.

The stakes were high for both sides. "If we're beaten like we were in 1960," said one shop steward with the International Union of Electrical Workers, "that's the end of the union at GE." Likewise, the strike sent ripples of fear through GE's managerial ranks and American boardrooms generally. Across the trenches, corporate officers saw their worst nightmare coming to life: Not only did the twelve-union alliance opposing GE bring together some of the most formidable personalities and organizations in labor's camp, it united once-bickering factions of the labor movement. There was, of course, the AFL-CIO's very mainstream president, George Meany; the maverick and leftish Walter Reuther; Paul Jennings of the IUE; and the quite radical James Matles of the United Electrical, Radio and Machine Workers. The UAW even kicked in more than a million dollars and a few veteran strategists and negotiators to aid the smaller electrical unions on their sectors of the front. Among the rank and file another frightening unity was forming: Along with the white, crew-cut old-school workers were legions of long-haired, pot-smoking youths, men and women, black and white, who unlike their elders did not recall the Depression and didn't fear the threats of GE's labor experts. The youth brought with them all the fury and iconoclasm of their generation—they were militant, pro-union, and ready to fight.

As Christmas 1969 came and went, the strike's economic impact reverberated through other industries. Eleven weeks of impasse at GE left Lear Jet holding a half-dozen executive jets in Wichita, Kansas with empty nacelles awaiting GE engines. Tecumseh's compressor-fabricating operations had no electric motors, forcing the company to lay off three hundred workers. Meanwhile, retailers began to feel the pinch as a boycott of GE consumer electronics and appliances gained momentum. Direct losses to GE were tallied at $100 million in missed profits.

On the picket lines the mood remained strangely calm.

Even in the company's Northeastern strongholds the press reported that strikers were settling in for the long haul with little of the anxiety seen during big strikes of years past. Why? To the horror of businessmen the answer soon arrived with all the sting of a shiv from Brutus. Strikers were not only receiving strike funds but tens of thousands of them were also drawing welfare checks! The government was subsidizing labor's side of the battle. "It's a mind-boggling situation," declared Thomas Litwiler, a GE executive in Pittsfield, Massachusetts. "The strikers are living reasonably well on welfare, and nobody knows what to do or what it really means any more." By the end of the victorious 122-day action, GE strikers had collected an estimated $25 million dollars in welfare. From the point of view of the employer class this was a disaster.

Welfare-subsidized class war, troubling enough in itself for the honchos at GE, was also a depressing barometer of larger problems. Working-class power was being institutionalized within the state, and the state in turn was being transformed. It seemed like the nation was creeping toward what conservatives liked to call collectivism.

Consider the fact that between 1964 and 1979 the federal government enacted sixty-two health and safety laws meant to protect workers and consumers, and thirty-two other laws to protect the environment and to regulate energy use. Many of these state interventions, it should be noted, were inaugurated during the Nixon administration. Between 1970 and 1973 Nixon presided over the creation of the Environmental Protection Agency, the Occupational Safety and Health Administration, the Consumer Safety Administration, and the Mine Enforcement and Safety Administration. The Brookings Institution estimated that by 1983 pollution controls alone had cost American business between $13 billion and $38 billion, and that measures to protect health and human safety cost between $7 billion and $17 billion.

Showdown 1970: Labor's Tet Offensive

LABOR's victory over GE presaged turbulent times to come. According to government statistics, contracts covering some five million workers would come up for nego-

corporate offensive launched against American workers in the early Seventies, however, is part of a different story: That was just business, and if it was often nasty business, that's just the way the world works. Of course, corporations funded politicians of both parties to gain influence, and the right-wing cultural and corporate agendas were linked in complex ways, in sync on some issues (like cutting taxes), offering opportunistic alliances on others (for example, businessmen were content to cloak their deregulatory agenda under gun nuts' populist anger against government). But as employers, as investors, and as business strategists, corporations were political in a broader sense that goes largely unrecognized: They fundamentally shifted the balance of social power in American life.

The New Deal and the rebirth of the labor movement in the Thirties and Forties had momentarily constrained the deeply rooted hostility of American big business leaders to workers, unions, and the government, but despite the hopeful illusions of some politicians, academics, and labor leaders about a new social accord, the old distrust and antagonism never really died. At their first opportunity with a congressional majority in 1947, Republicans pushed through the Taft-Hartley Act, which weakened unions, expanded employer rights, and advanced the bureaucratization of labor relations. Although they continued to fund attacks on labor, however, most big corporations either learned to live with unions or at least to mimic their contracts and grievance procedures as a means to discourage unionization. In the era of prosperity and global dominance following the Second World War, American corporations often grudgingly acceded to the wage increases and benefits that unions demanded, and

unions came to believe they could at least count on a détente in the class war. But by the early Seventies, American business executives felt under siege. Profits had dropped by a third from their peak of the mid-Sixties. The first pressures of low-priced foreign competition were hitting industries like electronics, apparel, textile, steel, and autos. Even Richard Nixon was compelled to endorse new regulations, such as the Occupational Safety and Health Act and the Clean Air Act. The country's boom, fueled in part by Johnson's strategy for financing the Vietnam War, produced the first concerns about inflation, which in turn helped to precipitate Nixon's later decision to break the link between gold and the dollar.

Then the first OPEC oil price shock hit. Since industry in the rest of the world was typically more energy-efficient, American businesses were hit especially hard. American productivity growth also lagged, but rather than invest heavily to raise the productivity of labor, improve product quality, and boost energy efficiency, business was more inclined to make employees pay for the squeeze on profits through reduced real incomes. While unions resisted and defended their cost-of-living agreements, nonunion workers suffered real wage losses. The gap between union and nonunion workers widened, with the union pay advantage over nonunion workers increasing by half during the Seventies. This undermined the already tenuous social and political cohesion of the working class and gave new incentives to employers to operate nonunion. Companies increasingly pursued "Southern strategies"—shifting

tiation in 1970, and unions were preparing to make significant wage demands. Employers braced for combat, and by the end of the year more than sixty-six million days of labor time would be lost to job actions, the highest toll due to strikes since the great postwar labor offensive of 1946.

As the storms of 1970 approached, the National Association of Manufacturers and the U.S. Chamber of Commerce sought to enlist the Nixon administration's help to impose labor discipline. But before long the federal government was embroiled in a labor-relations shitstorm of its own: On March 18 more than a thousand angry letter carriers in New York City dropped their bags and grabbed placards. Twenty-five thousand drivers and clerks honored the pickets, and within hours postal operations in New York City ground to a halt.

The action was illegal: Just for walking out each striker faced a possible felony charge carrying a minimum prison sentence of a year and a day along with a $1,000 fine. A federal court immediately imposed an injunction ordering postal employees to return to work, while James Rademacher, head of the national postal union, issued bellicose back-to-work orders of his own and made solemn promises to the postmaster general that the mail would move—rain, shine, or picket sign.

It didn't matter. Within two days the New York wildcat strike had spread across the country. Along with banners the strikers now carried effigies of "Rat-macher." In all, more than 200,000 of the nation's 740,000 postal workers were out in more than two hundred towns and cities. Hundreds of thousands of drivers and clerks halted before even the flimsiest of the letter carriers' picket lines. By March 21 the U.S. mails had completely stalled. "We're very close to paralysis," a postal official complained. "What is still functioning is hardly worthy of calling a postal system."

As local after local joined the strike, panic set in among opinion-makers and business leaders, and the press predicted a national "disaster." Nixon went on television to plead with the nation that nothing less was at stake than "the survival of a government based upon law." To restore order and move the mails he called out the armed forces. But even these scabs in olive drab displayed a voguish lack of discipline: Of the twenty-six thousand National Guard, Army, and Air Force reservists ordered to report for duty, only sixteen thousand showed up—and, according to *Newsweek*, many of those "got mixed reviews as postal workers," preferring to grab empty mail bags and "disappear for the day." Others fraternized openly with the strikers.

The worst-case scenario was unfolding. *Time*, in a perceptive assessment of the situation, warned that "the government's authority was placed in question and the well-being of business, institutions, and individuals in jeopardy." The price of order, it seemed, would have to be surrender to wildcat postmen who were demanding amnesty and a 40 percent raise in pay.

After a week without mail, negotiations had begun and the strikers returned to work, but they remained defiant. "It's got to be good and it's got to be quick," one letter carrier said of the talks in Washington, D.C. "Otherwise, we'll stay out till we get the money." In material terms the postal strike was a modest success: All government workers won an immediate 6 percent pay raise, and postal workers carried off an additional 8 percent on top of that. Politically, though, the impact of the strike was enormous, increasing the momentum that resulted from the ass-whooping administered to GE months earlier. The postal strike whetted working folks' appetite for struggle: No longer did workers need to cower before the bosses or Uncle Sam. "We've learned from the postal workers that if practically everybody strikes, then nobody is going to get hurt," one government worker told the *Washington Star*. "They can't fire everyone."

Almost immediately state and municipal workers started striking for better wages and more control on the job. Teachers, garbagemen, gravediggers, hospital workers, cops, and city office workers walked off the job in huge illegal strikes. Even the skies grew calm: Air traffic controllers, recently organized into the two-year-old Professional Air Traffic Controllers Organization (PATCO), called a rolling sick-out and threatened an illegal strike. Just as the postal strike was winding down PATCO's chief, attorney F. Lee Bailey, announced that the issue was safety, and that unless the union's demands were met the controllers would "shut down the air

production to nonunion states. Once companies proved they could aggressively break strikes using "permanent replacement workers," they found they could call on even lower-paid workers to cross picket lines in union strongholds like Austin, Minnesota, Jay, Maine, or Decatur, Illinois. In the late Seventies, unionized blue chip corporations joined their more vocal lesser brethren in defeating a modest union-led effort to reform labor laws. It provoked UAW President Doug Fraser to denounce the "one-sided class war" that corporations had launched. It has remained one-sided for much too long.

American corporations faced a choice in the Seventies: They could have offered workers more secure jobs, incomes, and retirement benefits in exchange for cooperation in boosting productivity—thus reducing inflation, restoring profits, cutting waste, and meeting international competition. Instead they chose to play a zero-sum game. "[I]t will be a hard pill for many Americans to swallow—the idea of doing with less so that big business can have more," as a *Business Week* reporter put it in a blunt analysis in late 1974. "Nothing that this nation, or any other nation, has done in modern economic history compares in difficulty with the selling job that must now be done to make people accept the new reality." It would be a hard pill indeed, considering that workers earning (and spending) more had long buttressed the popular legitimacy of the American system, particularly since the flower-

U.S. MAIL

ing of consumer-oriented capitalism in the Twenties. In 1959, when he faced Khrushchev in the famous "kitchen debate" at an American exhibit in Moscow, Nixon gibed that in the United States even a steelworker could own a house with new appliances like those on display. The ability of American capitalism to deliver the goods in the market probably counted more during the Cold War than the rhetoric about freedom and democracy, about which Americans had at best ambiguous feelings in practice.

Yet while American workers were at the top of the international heap in the Fifties, in the Seventies their edge began to slip. Depending on how wage statistics are adjusted for currency exchange rates, the average manufacturing worker in at least six—or as many as eleven—countries made more than American production workers in 1996, according to the Economic Policy Institute. Popular rhetoric shifted from extolling American greatness to public hand-wringing about America's loss of "competitiveness." Rather than recognize their own managerial shortcomings—such as failing to design high-quality goods, invest in the most advanced technology, or cut bloated, unproductive managerial overhead—American managers typically blamed their own workers. Looking overseas, they thought they were at a disadvantage because American workers were expensive (even though they often continued to lose the competitive battle in the Eighties and Nineties when the United States turned into a comparatively low-wage industrial country). They too wanted cheap workers, so they headed South or overseas and shifted production to

traffic system." PATCO won its pay increase and other concessions without having to go that far.

Due to strikes in the construction trades, many cities suffered industry-wide work halts for weeks at time. In Kansas City commercial construction projects were halted for more than three months. "There are very widespread strikes in construction," commented a perturbed Secretary of Labor George Shultz. "Settlements are coming in. They are at extremely high levels. They're higher than last year, which was an extraordinary year. . . . This is a formula for disaster."

In what would become a trademark phrase of the era, William W. Winpisinger, Machinists president and chief negotiator for the angry railroad unions, described his rank and file as "running right on the edge of being out of control." Far from making threats, he was pleading with employers to help him maintain power. It was a common theme. Everywhere one looked workers were spoiling for a fight. By the early Seventies labor leaders had to learn to fight on two fronts: After squeezing concessions from employers it was not uncommon for even generous contracts to be rejected by the pugnacious rank and file. By 1971 it was estimated that 15 percent of all contracts were being rejected, up from around 8 percent in 1964. At the UAW Reuther even took to staging small strikes just to placate his action-hungry and increasingly youthful rank and file.

But one contract rejected by angry Teamsters trumped all others. The trouble began on April Fools' Day 1970, after what was described as "the most orderly" series of contract negotiations in Teamster history. The independent union's new president, Frank Fitzsimmons, had won his truckers a $1.10 per-hour wage increase, but the rank and file wanted sick pay and wouldn't take the contract. Immediately drivers walked in sixteen cities, including the key hubs of Los Angeles, San Francisco, Cleveland, Atlanta, Chicago, Detroit, Buffalo and Milwaukee. In the Midwest, the strategic chokepoint of the strike, renegade locals set up mobile pickets and blockades. Trucks moving east found most key crossing points on the Mississippi occupied by huge squads of wildcat Teamsters. Only trucks carrying food, medicine, and beer were allowed to move. Trucks that tried to smuggle other products underneath loads of soup or behind racks of beef wound up with smashed windshields, slashed tires, and sabotaged engines. As freight movement ground to a halt across the country, layoffs in other industries began to mount. Within a week an estimated half-million workers were directly or indirectly idled by the Teamsters' wildcat. Greyhound, the airlines, and inland river barges all increased their freight volume exponentially, but it did little to fill the breach. As stranded merchandise piled up in poorly guarded heaps, manufacturers and wholesalers reported expensive waves of theft.

Fitzsimmons, the employers, and the courts closed rank against the outlaw strikers. In state after state injunctions rained down from hostile courts, employers swore no compromise and union leaders did all they could to force the drivers back on the road. The governor of Ohio called out the 145th Infantry, the same National Guard Unit that had just gunned down students at Kent State and put down several urban riots, to escort small convoys of scab-driven trucks. None of it worked. After twelve weeks, trucking firms in Chicago capitulated to the wildcatters' demands. With that the employer unity crumbled, and the Teamsters won their right to sick pay.

Meanwhile, in coal country wildcat strikes were becoming epidemic. As *Fortune* magazine put it, management faced "a work force that is no longer under union discipline." Among the miners' grievances were the industry's abysmal health and safety standards. In 1969 miners in West Virginia had begun what was called the Black Lung Wildcat. Within days nearly all of the state's forty-four thousand miners had dropped their tools. After twenty-three days in which no coal came up from the shafts, the state legislature passed a law compensating three thousand victims of coal dust pneumoconiosis. But it wasn't enough. For the next two years wildcat strikes continued in the mines. Nineteen thousand Pennsylvania miners walked in 1970, protesting lack of enforcement of new safety rules; fifteen thousand miners staged another wildcat in West Virginia to demand hospital benefits for disabled miners and their widows. Under union bylaws the rank and file had long been denied the right to vote on

nonunion plants. When they couldn't flee, they fought, taking advantage of the deep recession of the early Eighties, for example, to demand concessions from workers even when their companies were quite profitable.

American business was already deeply committed to what the late economist David M. Gordon called the "Stick" strategy (which he contrasts to the "Carrot" strategy, based on more cooperative workplace relations). In his 1996 book, *Fat and Mean*, Gordon demonstrated how the "bureaucratic burden" of excessive supervisory and managerial personnel in American companies has grown dramatically since the end of the Second World War and remains several times greater than among leading industrial countries with more cooperative labor relations. In the Forties and Fifties corporate bureaucracy grew rapidly as American business attempted to gain tighter control over its work force. The ratio of managers to production workers leveled off somewhat in the Sixties, then shot up again in the early Seventies before leveling off in the mid-Eighties. By 1989 the bureaucratic burden on U.S. corporations was about 3.6 times that of the average firm in Germany, Japan, and Sweden. The American model of surveillance and discipline became more top-heavy in part because in such a distrustful system even the monitors needed monitoring.

As Gordon maintained, Stick systems underperform Carrot systems on several counts—productivity, competitiveness, wages, hours of work. But when the crunch came in the early Seventies, American business merely expanded their managerial apparatus. They stuck with the Stick strategy because it was what they knew and it reinforced their wealth and power. But it was also true that individual companies could sometimes make short-term gains by cracking down on their workers, even if it was counterproductive in the long term. Despite the chaotic and counterproductive strategy of downsizing in recent years, Gordon found the bureaucratic burden has changed little and is still many times greater than in countries where management is less hostile to workers, in part because workers there are better organized and have more political leverage, but also because of cultural differences in both managerial circles and the country at large. The irony, Gordon noted, is that the intensification of authoritarian strategies over the past twenty-five years undermined productivity, thus pushing corporations to use an even bigger Stick.

The corporate crackdown on workers extended beyond union-busting, concession bargaining, speed-ups, lockouts, subcontracting, and other assaults on workers. It undermined the minimum wage, attacked regulation, and promoted the use of contingent workers (such as temps and part-timers). It not only moved production outside the United States, but also used the mere threat to do so to bust unions and otherwise discipline workers. It entailed Federal Reserve policies that created recessions and kept unemployment high—all in the name of fighting inflation—even when wages were not driving inflation. It created new markets in corporate control, as raiders like Kohlberg Kravis Roberts & Co. challenged the power of corporate executives and demanded higher stock prices, even if their takeovers or the defenses against them led to massive layoffs and looted pension plans to pay

their own contracts. By 1972, after years of internecine strife and bloodshed, insurgent miners had overthrown union despot Tony Boyle and democratized the United Mine Workers. They also won significant wage increases from the mine owners.

In 1972, after five years of boycott and strikes, the United Farm Workers had finally brought the last of the table grape growers to heel and signed contracts with all of them. The next year brought more strikes nationwide: Five hundred thousand walked out at Bell Telephone; commercial fishermen in New Bedford, Massachusetts, the fourth largest fishing port in the nation, refused to work; the railroads were hassled by sporadic and ongoing labor action; even workers at Disneyland planned a strike. As fifteen thousand striking longshoremen paralyzed the West Coast all summer and into autumn, the governor of Oregon described the strike as a "nightmare." Forest products piled up, mills prepared to close, and wheat was dumped on the ground for lack of storage or transportation facilities. After ninety-eight days Nixon forced the West Coast longshoremen back to work with a Taft-Hartley injunction, but by that point they had been joined by forty thousand comrades on the Gulf and the East Coast. Eventually the combination of spreading rail strikes and the longshoremen's bicoastal lockdown forced thousands of layoffs in other industries.

The Informal Fight

B ESIDES staging wildcat strikes, restive workers increasingly resorted to informal rebellion on the shop floor. Ford Motor Co. claimed that absenteeism in its plants doubled and sometimes even tripled during the Sixties and early Seventies. In one factory workers wrote messages to management on their machinery, such as, "Treat me with respect and I will give you top quality with less effort." As Michael Perelman points out in *The Pathology of the U.S. Economy*, the countercultural zeitgeist's new emphasis on creativity and freedom—combined with the cultural chaos and cynicism generated by the war, riots, and police repression—began to express itself on the shop floor as mass insubordination. Sabotage, slowdowns, and wildcats became the industrial equivalent of "fragging" officers in Vietnam (where many of the young malcontents no doubt first learned to disobey). In *The Reckoning*, David Halberstam describes the plight of a Ford manager in a plant plagued with absenteeism and sabotage. Among the plant's employees was a young man who consistently skipped work on Friday or Monday. When the manager finally demanded to know why he worked a four-day week the young man replied, "Because I can't make a living working three days a week." He spoke for a generation; working-class power translated into an informal economy-wide slowdown, which meant a measured decline in productivity.

An article in *Radical America* from the Seventies gave an almost utopian account of a year on the insurgent shop floors of Detroit. The so-called "counterplanning" by workers included pooling break time and covering work stations so that instead of short breaks workers could have longer, extended rests. Sabotage was rampant, conducted as revenge against tyrannical foremen or in a methodical and organized fashion so as to ensure ample downtime. When the weather got hot, work occasionally took a back seat to water fights and horseplay. In his 1972 book *Strike!* Jeremy Brecher noted that much of this shop floor resistance was aimed at gaining control over the production process. Toward that end, UAW locals made thirty-nine thousand demands on GM in 1970 alone, for such things as greater control over shift schedules and work assignments, more vacation time, better wash-up facilities, legal advice, subsidized auto repair, and in-plant child care.

The Scales of Class Power, Tipped

THERE are many ways to measure working-class power. One is what economist Juliet Schor calls "the cost of job loss"—that is, the amount of income, measured in terms of potentially missed wages, that the average worker loses between jobs. When the cost of job loss is high (e.g., when unemployment benefits are reduced, or when welfare benefits slashed or restricted), workers will be less likely to risk be-

stockholders more. It promoted management fads, such as downsizing, which often did more to destroy morale and productivity than they did to cut costs. It imposed a "Washington consensus" on global trade and finance, in effect exporting the Corporate Stick strategy to countries already trying to emerge from under the rule of other sticks in the hands of generals and dictators. Above all, the corporate backlash has enshrined the ideology of market society, where, to paraphrase journalist Robert Kuttner, if everything isn't for sale, it sure ought to be. The "magic of the market" promised infinite freedom of choice for consumers and the liberation of entrepreneurial fulfillment, but the reality of the market was more often shrinking paychecks, more debt, and unpredictable, part-time, temporary work for the new hunters and gatherers picking amid the glitter of "the new economy." While the market fundamentalists rhapsodized about freedom, corporations were stealthily pursuing and gaining more and more power.

One result in the United States has been a growing inequality, with the increasingly bloated managerial class, along with a tiny stratum of stockholders, capturing virtually all of the economic gains of the past twenty-five years, while the incomes of the bottom four-fifths of American working families have either fallen or stagnated, sustained only by more family members working harder and longer. This growing inequality has little to do with the unequal distribution of education and skills—contrary to what we're so often told—and much to do with the skewed distribution of power.

Yet the corporate class's power grab, which should be the center of American political debate, is taboo in the mainstream media. Pundits remark perplexedly about how confused the political spectrum is these days in America, how it's hard to tell who's on the left or right (which they typically define in terms of social issues, such as prayer in schools and abortion). Democrats figure they can win elections by craftily focusing on a few of these issues; they applaud Clinton for cleverly "taking away" the issues of crime and capital punishment from the Republicans. But during eight years in office, Clinton has never once talked about how workers deserve the "free choice"—free especially of interference from the boss—about whether they want a union. While his administration shortchanged the United Nations, neglected aid to impoverished countries, and promoted destructive austerity for poor nations, Clinton turned foreign policy into a trade mission for American business. Only during his first presidential campaign (and then later after he lost his bid for "fast track" trade negotiating authority) did Clinton talk about the need to protect workers' rights in global trade deals—even though he still promoted legislation like the "Nafta for Africa" bill that did little to protect African workers. After letting the real value of the minimum wage shrivel to its lowest level in five decades, Clinton only belatedly pushed for a modestly higher minimum wage when it became politically expedient. While willing to spar modestly with the cultural right, the Clintonian "third way" in politics resolutely ignores—or even embraces—the triumph of corporate power.

Thanks to the success of their agenda, corporations feel less need these days to court their sometimes distasteful partners in the cultural backlash. They will win with Gore or Bush, even if they prefer Bush. Meanwhile, many of those who once were or still are conservative cultural populists—pundits Kevin Phillips

ing fired for militant labor activity—and so their power is reduced. Another indicator is the ratio of quits to layoffs and quits to job openings. When more employees quit than are laid off or fired, one can conclude that employers have lost a degree of control over the work force. That is exactly what happened during the late Sixties and early Seventies: The ratio of quits to layoffs reached two to one, almost twice what it was in the late Fifties. The share of the work force involved in some strike activity between 1967 and 1973 reached 40 percent—even though in the same period the unemployment rate crept from 4 to 8 percent.

What terrified businessmen in the early Seventies was not just that the price of labor was going up, but that it was going up regardless of unemployment rates. As the American economy cooled and slid into recession in 1973, the unemployment rate pitched upward, and yet wages and prices did not fall in response. This combination of stagnant growth and rising inflation became known as "stagflation."

The historically consistent inverse relationship between wage levels and unemployment is known among economists as the "Phillips Curve." For the first time in American history the two components of this economic "law" were out of whack. This led in part to a precipitous decline in the general rate of profit. In *The Great U-Turn*, Bennett Harrison and Barry Bluestone explain, "From a peak of nearly 10 percent in 1965, the average net after-tax profit rate of domestic non-financial corporations plunged to less than 6 percent during the second half of the Seventies—a decline of more than a third." The nadir was 1974, when the general rate of profit reached a low of around 4.5 percent. Throughout the rest of the Seventies inflation and unemployment persisted, labor unrest continued, and profits stagnated. Workers were claiming an unprecedented share of the wealth they produced. It was an unmitigated disaster for those who owned, and they would soon take terrible revenge.

The profit crisis was not fully resolved until 1979, when President Jimmy Carter gave in to the monetarist consensus among economists and appointed Paul Volcker as chairman of the Federal Reserve Board. Now it was capital's turn to "shut it down." Within months of taking office Volcker dramatically boosted interest rates, thus cutting borrowing and buying power, and chilling economic activity in general. Reagan accelerated this monetarist squeeze when he took office: Interest rates actually reached 16.4 percent in 1981. As a direct result, the United States plunged into its most severe recession since the Thirties. The plan was simple: Punish uppity American workers with a "cold bath" recession and they would learn to work harder for less. "The standard of living of the average American has to decline," Volcker told the *New York Times* in 1979. "I don't think you can escape that."

The war on labor, it was hoped—added to Reagan's proposals to cut taxes for the rich, to gut welfare, and to deregulate health, safety, and environmental standards—would boost corporate profits back to comfortable levels. But getting to yes would take time. In 1981, as the recession was reaching new depths, many in Congress began to lose their nerve and called for relief. Volcker again explained the utility of his artificial economic disaster: "[I]n an economy like ours with wages and salaries accounting for two-thirds of all costs, sustaining progress [in price reduction] will need to be reflected in moderation of growth of nominal wages. The general indexes of worker compensation still show relatively little improvement, and prices of many services with high labor content continue to show high rates of increase." The recession—though hard on many businesses, particularly small firms—had not yet achieved its purpose: wages were still rising.

Not until 1982, when Continental Illinois Bank began to collapse under the weight of its bad loans, did Volcker relent and open the Fed's spigots. By then the deep recession had worked its magic: Ten million people were unemployed by 1982, and the press was

and Pat Buchanan, and presidential candidate Gary Bauer, for example—have begun to regard the corporate ascendancy as a threat to the average American family. At the same time, unions and many economic populists resent the Democratic Party's reluctance to embrace the constructive role of government and to redress the injustices of the market and the growing tyranny of the workplace. Parts of the political left have occasionally allied with the anti-globalization right to block new international initiatives, but there is little chance that they will come together on many positive goals. Maybe Butch eventually could be persuaded to join a union and fight for single-payer health insurance, but until he is ready to scrape off his bumper stickers (or his economic populist allies decide to tolerate them), the culture wars will continue to serve the needs of its uneasy senior partner as it applies the Stick to Butch's behind.

running stories on the "new poor." Wage reductions became the norm in contract negotiations. Weekly take-home pay fell more than 8 percent between 1979 and 1982 and failed to recover for the next five years. But the most amazing measure of the recession's political success was this simple fact: Before the 1980–82 recession, wage freezes and pay cuts in unionized industries had been almost nonexistent. In 1980 not a single union contract negotiation had ended in a pay freeze or cut. By 1982, however, 44 percent of new contracts conceded wage freezes or outright cuts. Wages had been rising more or less consistently since the end of the Second World War, but now the tide had turned.

But macroeconomic medicine went only so far. Reagan began stacking the National Labor Relations Board, the federal body which arbitrates labor disputes, with anti-union activists. The courts, too, were salted with union-hating judges. To really put labor back in its place the Reagan administration chose a direct confrontation. When PATCO struck in 1981, Reagan instantly fired all eleven thousand striking controllers, never mind the fact that they had endorsed him during the election. This massacre sent a clear signal: The war was on and the government would back business to the hilt.

The Reagan administration also sanctioned the use of contingent labor; it even set an example in 1985 by allowing the government to hire temp workers at below union wages. Then in 1986 the Reagan administration legalized home work, a practice many trade unions argued would lead to exploitation and child labor and would undermine established minimum levels of health and safety. That is exactly what happened. According to Harley Shaiken, the doyen of labor studies, the U.S. Labor Department reported twenty thousand child-labor-law violations in 1988, up from thirteen thousand in 1986. There was a *500 percent increase* in the number of New York City sweatshops employing children. The number of minors illegally employed in sweatshops *increased 128 percent* nationwide in the second half of the Eighties.

So it is today. It is easy for us mortals to forget this legacy of the Sixties and Seventies, but others never will. For capital those years brought a glimpse, however abstract, of its own mortality. It was the nightmare that has spurred the right-wing backlash ever since, as the fear of falling rides the collective psyche of the business class like some tenacious and leering incubus. To keep the horror at bay, the leaders of the rich deploy their policy amulets and political mojos: ruthless austerity for those who toil; constant racist demagoguery; paranoid and irrelevant moralizing; and always more cops, more laws, more prison, and more discipline for working people.